SOUTHERN VOICES FROM THE PAST

Women's Letters, Diaries, and Writings

This series makes available to scholars, students, and general

readers collections of letters, diaries, and other writings by

women in the southern United States from the colonial era

into the twentieth century. Documenting the experiences of

women from across the region's economic, cultural, and ethnic

spectrums, the writings enrich our understanding of such

aspects of daily life as courtship and marriage, domestic life

and motherhood, social events and travels, and religion and

education.

Chained *to the* Rock *of* Adversity

r welcom letter and was happy
I family is injoying good health
now leaves myself and sisters a
ister is very well and is going no
house to play Ellen was hear ye
evening with us. I received the
gown for cathrien and the pe
much oblige to you. I have sent
by jeff I had not time to go
but I will send it next trip.
all the children. give my love to
ldren emma had not time to wr
joe for me and alice. give my l
waiting for my letter if you r
had not time to answer her letter
nent week I heard mag was to b
it is it true - I must stop.
more at present I remain
er neice   Clarinia Muller y
broke old Mrs coalmans neck

 Chained

to the

Rock *of*

Adversity

To Be Free, Black &

Female in the Old South

Edited by Virginia Meacham Gould

The University of Georgia Press

Athens and London

© 1998 by the
University of Georgia Press
Athens, Georgia 30602
All rights reserved
Designed by Richard Hendel
Set in Minion by G & S Typesetters, Inc.
Printed and bound by Maple-Vail
The paper in this book meets the
guidelines for permanence and durability
of the Committee on Production Guidelines for
Book Longevity of the Council on Library Resources.
Printed in the United States of America
02 01 00 99 98   C   5 4 3 2 1
Library of Congress Cataloging in Publication Data
Chained to the rock of adversity : to be free, Black &
female in the Old South / edited by Virginia
Meacham Gould.
p.   cm. — (Southern voices from the past)
Includes bibliographical references and index.
ISBN 0-8203-1996-1 (alk. paper). — ISBN 0-8203-
2083-8 (pbk. : alk. paper)
1. Afro-American women—Mississippi—Natchez
Region—History—19th century—Sources.
2. Afro-American women—Louisiana—New
Orleans Region—History—19th century—Sources.
3. Afro-American women—Mississippi—Natchez
Region—Social life and customs—Sources.
4. Afro-American women—Louisiana—New
Orleans Region—Social life and customs—Sources.
5. Free Afro-Americans—Mississippi—Natchez
Region—History—19th century—Sources.
6. Free Afro-Americans—Louisiana—New Orleans
Region—History—19th century—Sources.
7. Natchez Region (Miss.)—Race relations—
Sources.   8. New Orleans Region (La.)—Race
relations—Sources.   9. Johnson family—Archives.
I. Gould, Virginia Meacham.   II. Series.
F349.N2C48   1998
976.2'2600496073—dc21   98-14341

British Library
Cataloging in Publication Data available

For my mother and father,

MARY HELEN SUMERLIN MEACHAM

and

CHARLES TILMAN MEACHAM

Contents

Preface

The letters and diary included here are unique among those of southern women. Unlike most other personal accounts that document the experiences and identities of one southern woman, these are the assembled writings of several women and a few men. The letters were written to two women, Ann Battles Johnson and her daughter Anna Johnson between 1844 and 1899. Most were from family members. A few were from friends, mostly women, and together the letters offer an entire chorus of women's voices. The diary was written by Catharine Geraldine Johnson — Ann's daughter and Anna's sister. The value of the writings in this volume lies not in their variety but in the extraordinary story they tell. It is the race, or condition, of the women who both wrote and received these letters and diary that makes the documents so valuable. The letters and diary in this remarkable collection are the only personal and private voices of free women of color that we have.

One of the women who emerges most clearly off the pages of these documents is Ann Battles Johnson, along with the patterns of her life, the rhythms of her days. It is from these pages that we learn that Ann's life indisputably echoes the gender conventions that bound southern women in the discreet relations and customs that defined the region. Indeed, the boundaries of Ann's life, her birth and her death, closely followed the rise and fall of the Old South. Born in 1815, Ann reached adulthood as the antebellum years began. In 1835 when she was twenty years old, Ann married the prosperous and dashing Natchez businessman William T. Johnson after six years of courtship. During the next sixteen years of her life, Ann bore ten children. Her last child, born in 1851, was just one month old when her husband died. It was at the death of her husband that Ann was thrust into the role of head of household, a role that she grew increasingly comfortable with until her death in 1866.

There were the notable events that punctuated Ann's life — her marriage, the birth of her children, her husband's death, the war. And certainly it was just those events that inextricably tied Ann to the nineteenth-century South, that placed her in a world in which women's roles were closely defined. Yet, it is not in those specific events nor in the roles that followed them that we find the significance of Ann's life. For that we must look to the dailiness of her existence. Evidence from the letters, the diary, and other sources demonstrates that Ann's days were filled with the often tedious yet sometimes overwhelming duties assigned to southern slaveholding women. Yet even as the nature of her roles as daughter and sister, wife and mother, slaveholder and household manager linked her inextricably to other women of the slaveholding class, her race — or skin color — separated her from it.

Ann Battles Johnson was a freed slave, a free woman of color. The letters that she and her daughter Anna received were from other free women of color, some of whom were also freed slaves; the others were from free men of color. The letters were mostly addressed to Ann and Anna at their home in Natchez and were mostly from their kin in New Orleans. A few letters were written by free people of color who lived in the plantation region that lay between Natchez and New Orleans. Catharine's diary was written at the family home in Natchez.

Perhaps Ann, Anna, and Catharine and the women who wrote to them knew that their experiences as free women of color in a society that defined slavery by race were significant. Perhaps they did not. Either way, they accumulated and jealously protected the letters they received from their family and friends and the diary in which Catharine so painstakingly bared her soul. Ann, Anna, and Catharine left their papers with those of their father in the attic of their home in Natchez. They remained there until 1938 when Mrs. Edith Wyatt Moore, a Natchez newspaperwoman heard about them. She contacted the widow of Dr. William R. Johnston, Ann Battles Johnson's grandson, in order to procure the documents. Mrs. Johnston eventually reached an agreement with Louisiana State University where the collection is now being carefully preserved.

Like thousands of other pages of women's writings, the letters and diaries reproduced here are included in a collection that is named for the patriarch of the family, William T. Johnson. William was a prosperous barber and planter, a free man of color in antebellum Natchez. The collection that bears his name is extensive, including more than 1,310 items. The majority of the documents are his. He left numerous journals, daybooks, ledgers, cashbooks, notebooks, and bankbooks. William began record-keeping in 1835 and continued until his untimely death in 1851. Most of what he noted concerned his business affairs, but he occasionally jotted down his observations about his personal life, his family, and the town of Natchez. Not only do his comments offer us glimpses into his daily activities, they enhance what we know about the lives of his wife and daughters.

The letters Ann and Anna received from their family and friends were

personal and private. None of the women ever intended for their correspondence to be read by others. Instead, each letter spoke to the depths of
the intimacy that knit the women together, one to the other. They tell of a
women's world that was filled with the humdrum of household duties and
children's demands. Yet despite their dailiness, the letters reveal intimate
details and provide a window into the lives of a remarkable group of
women.

In their entirety, the women's letters span the years 1844 to 1936. Only
those letters written between 1844 and 1899 are included here. Catharine's
diary was begun in 1864. She continued writing in it, on rare occasions,
until 1874. Taken together the documents cover a period during which the
South experienced immense change. The letters divide naturally into two
sections. The first, which includes the letters penned between 1844 and 1866
were written to Ann. The later ones, written after Ann died in 1866, were
written to her daughter, Anna.

Most of the early letters were from William's sister, Adelia Johnson Miller of New Orleans and her daughters Emma, Octavia, and Lavinia. Occasionally Adelia wrote her brother, William, instead of Ann. Others were
from Ann's and William's sons who were also living in New Orleans. Few
of the letters are particularly striking in content. They mostly contain evidence of day-to-day concerns of the women who wrote them and of the
women who received them. We already know much about the daily experiences of southern white women, about how they viewed their world and
how they related to others in it. We even know something about the lives
and experiences of slave women. Very little, however, is known about the
world of free women of color. The letters included here, when read within
the broader political and social context of their era, tell a story of the South
that was unique, a story of a community of women who had escaped from
slavery and yet continued to feel its weight, no matter how far they got away
from it.

The early letters were written and received by free men and women of
color whose very existences threatened the ideological basis of slavery and
the southern social hierarchy. They were received by women who inter-
acted daily with the white and slave communities of Natchez — they were
even related by blood to the white and slave communities and yet were
accepted into neither. The free women of color writing these letters found
themselves in a public world that they both threatened and were threatened
by. Their letters offer ample evidence that they protected their identities
and thus their status by limiting their association to those within their own

narrow social group (those free people of color who were tied together by condition) and to whites who were tied to the community of free people of color through kinship.

The letters written between 1866 and 1899 reveal a very different world from the one the women knew before the Civil War. After Ann's death in 1866, Anna took her mother's place as head of household, thus the later letters were addressed to her. Some of the letters to Anna were from friends, but most were from her brothers and sisters. The letters written to Anna from her siblings tell a poignant tale of a family that suffered continuing economic decline after the war. Before the war was over, Anna and her sisters took turns baking pies that they sold in town and at the docks. They turned to sharecropping, hiring some of their ex-slaves as laborers. After finally admitting failure at sharecropping, they put their educations to work by teaching freed people and their children to read and to write, to add and subtract, to know something about the world around them.

The diary of Catharine Geraldine Johnson continues the family story. Catharine was born in 1843; she was Ann and William's sixth child, their third daughter. Catharine began her diary during the Civil War and wrote in it sporadically for the next ten years. Perhaps the tragedy of the war inspired Catharine to keep a diary. Maybe she recognized that the war would bring great change to her life and that of her kin and that by keeping a diary she would be able to understand the change. She might have begun to keep a diary in order to identify more closely with her father who had kept one. Maybe she even had aspirations to be a writer or a poet. Her diary is filled with examples of her poetry and prose, much of it dedicated to her father.

While the women's documents included here have been virtually ignored, those of free men of color have not. In 1951, William's journals were published under the title *William Johnson's Natchez* and edited by William Ransom-Hogan and Edwin Adams Davis. In 1954 Edwin Davis published *The Barber of Natchez,* which examined the social, political, and economic experiences of William Johnson. Another collection of documents of free people of color is the letters of the Ellison family of South Carolina, which offer a glimpse into the experiences of free people along the eastern seaboard. The letters, edited by Michael P. Johnson and James L. Roark and collected in *No Chariot Let Down,* are mostly written from Charleston. They offer meaning by tracing Ellison's daily lives in the midst of the increasing threats from the white ruling class.

A world profound with meaning lies between the lines of the letters and diary of this collection. But that world is not obvious. It lies hidden behind the routines of the women who wrote the letters and those who read them. Therefore, the documents cannot stand alone. They must be read within the context of what we know about the nineteenth-century South and its place within nineteenth-century America. Yet even that is not enough. In order to understand the day-to-day adversities and joys of the free women of color, to understand their extreme marginalization and the choices they made because of it, we must read the pages reproduced here within the context of other research. William Johnson's diary sheds light on much of what is missing from these pages. Legal statutes, court and property records, and sacramental records suggest the restrictive world of the Johnsons and their neighbors and kin on the Mississippi and Louisiana deltas.

When first shown the letters and diary in Baton Rouge, I was overwhelmed by their importance. So few documents of free people of color are available to us today that I had little hope of finding more than just a letter or two. Yet as I read through the collection within which these papers are included, I realized that I had finally found a compelling chronicle of a remarkable group of women who lived in the region. These records give us more than just a hint of the variety of experiences that women of color and black women found in nineteenth-century America.

The documents offer the reader a powerful statement in their original state. The penmanship tells much about the personalities of the women. Catharine filled her diary with doodles. Many times she seems to have been stuck on a phrase or a line of a poem, writing it over and over. At times, her jottings seemed to constitute a plea, either to herself or to a greater being. Some of the letters contain secret messages written sideways between the lines or jotted in code at the bottom of a page. The reminiscences and the messages in the letters and diary tell as much about the women and how they felt about their world as the main context of their pennings. In order to retain the original character of the letters and diary for the reader I have followed simple guidelines. Misspellings are common and usually obvious, therefore I have not attempted to standardize them. Capitalization and punctuation, both of which are placed randomly throughout the text offer more serious problems for the reader. In order to make the documents more accessible, I have added capitals at the beginning of each sentence and a period at the end.

To understand the women who wrote these pages it is necessary to place them within their world, particularly because it did not represent the dominant structures that surrounded them. The women knew themselves to be in precarious roles, feared and poorly tolerated by many of their white neighbors and resented by their slaves. The early letters hint at the ways in which the women related to their slave and white neighbors, how their private political views were translated into public action. They give evidence to a tight-knit network of family and friends that reached hundreds of miles up and down the Mississippi River. Catharine's diary and the later letters suggest a difficult transition through the period of the war and after, a time during which the women should have been forming their own families but instead were driven to earn wages out of economic necessity. There are far more stories between the lines of these pages than can be captured here, but I have tried to set the stage for the reader to hear the voices of these extraordinary women.

❧ Acknowledgments

While the unyielding support of so many scholars, archivists, friends, and family members makes the task of acknowledgment nearly impossible, it also makes it even more important. Faye Phillips of Special Collections at Hill Memorial Library, Louisiana State University introduced me to the letters and diary that appear in this collection. Faye recognized that the documents that had been viewed as an indistinct part of the William T. Johnson Collection were, in their own right, unique and thus should be published as such. To Faye and to her always helpful staff, I offer my special thanks.

I must also thank Elaine Smith and Judy Bolton of Hill Memorial Library; they generously provided me with the materials that made this book possible.

Stuart Johnson and his successor Kathleen Jenkins of the Natchez National Historic Park have been especially helpful. They have unselfishly shared what they know of the Johnson-Miller family and directed me toward archives and other resources in Natchez. They also introduced me to Ron and Mimi Miller of the Natchez Historic Foundation. Ron and Mimi know all there is to know about Natchez.

I fear that I can only attempt to acknowledge my debt of gratitude to the many historians and archivists in New Orleans who have generously shared their knowledge and expertise with me over the years. Each and every one has contributed immeasurably to my education in the history of the region. Wayne Everard, Colin Hamer, and Irene Wainwright of the Louisiana Division of the New Orleans Public Library have patiently led me through the library's immense holdings. Sally Reeves of the city's notarial archives has spent years helping me track down property records for free women of color. She continues to lead me toward an understanding of women as property holders in the city. Pamela Arseneaux of the Historic New Orleans Collection was always there with suggestions. She, as well as many of the other staff members, have generously shared their time and knowledge with me. I must also thank Marie Wendell, the archivist of Special Collections, the University of New Orleans. Marie is a walking encyclopedia of the Supreme Court records of Louisiana that are located at the University.

There are no words to adequately thank Archbishop Oscar Lipscomb for his support. He opened the archives of the Cathedral of the Immaculate

Conception to me and also shared his vast knowledge of the history of the region. Charles Nolan, Archdiocesan Archivist for the Archdiocese of New Orleans, assisted in making the sacramental records of the St. Louis Cathedral available to me. He and his wife, Gayle, became cherished friends in the process.

So many historians encouraged me to get on with my work that it is impossible to thank them all here. Special thanks must be given to Catherine Clinton and Carol Bleser who immediately recognized the value of these papers and encouraged me through the process. There are many other scholars who have urged me along the way, including, to name a few, Gwendolyn Hall, Paul LaChance, Kimberly Hanger, Kent Leslie, Patricia Morton, Wilma King, Darlene Clark Hine, Barry Gaspar, Jim Dorman, Suzanne White Junod, and Lisa Tyree. They would not allow me to quit.

I must especially thank my many mentors in the history department at Emory University. Harvey Young took me under his wing when I returned to graduate school. He gave generously of his time, reassuring me that graduate school was "not just for one type of person." John Jurecek taught me my love for colonial history at the same time that he guided me through the mysteries of graduate requirements. Jim Roark and Dan Carter taught me to know and appreciate the many Souths that I did not know. Susan Socolow enlarged my understanding of southern history by carefully leading me from the South, which I knew and loved, into the world of Latin America and the Caribbean. As I reconsidered, under her tutorage, what I knew about the Gulf region, I came to understand it as a part of a much larger western world. Susan became a valued friend as she pushed me to broaden my thinking. It is to these professors who taught me the importance of history that this, my first book, belongs.

I owe a debt of gratitude to Patrick McKee and Katherine Burge-Calloway that can never be repaid. They gave me the courage to write this book.

Finally, I owe an immeasurable amount of gratitude to my husband, Jeffrey, and my sons Marc, Mitchell, Jeremy, and Grahame. They have always been my biggest fans, despite the many sacrifices they have had to make along the way.

As head of household, one of Ann Battles Johnson's responsibilities was corresponding with her family and friends. Letter writing was a duty she took seriously. And even though most women learned such duties as letter writing from their mothers, she did not. Her mother, Harriett Battles, could neither read nor write.[1] She had been a slave and had been denied the opportunity to develop such skills. Although Ann had also been born into slavery, she had acquired the skills of reading and writing. Perhaps she taught herself. Perhaps her master saw to it that she had a rudimentary education. Either way, by the time she was grown, Ann had acquired an education, and she made certain that her children acquired one also. It was Ann who supervised her children's educations and encouraged her daughters to take their letter-writing skills seriously. Ann knew that the letters that she wrote and those that she received from her kin knit the family together in a familiar day-to-day fashion.

Unfortunately, the early letters (those dated before 1866) were not written by Ann or her daughters. It appears that those letters have not survived. Instead, the letters included in this volume were written to Ann by her sister-in-law, Adelia Johnson Miller, and her daughters Emma, Lavinia, and Octavia Miller. The letters are responses to Ann's letters. The letters that Adelia and her daughters wrote to Ann were never very long, rarely even a page each. Nor were they very polished. Oftentimes, they were little more than an apology for not having written sooner or for not having the time to write more. But the letters they did write, those letters that Ann Battles Johnson so carefully saved, offer substantive and invaluable evidence of their experiences and attitudes, evidence of the women in their roles as daughters, nieces, sisters, wives, and mothers.

The letters that sailed up and down the Mississippi River between Natchez and New Orleans tied the Johnson side of the family (that of Ann and her daughters) in Natchez with that of the Millers (that of Adelia and her daughters) of New Orleans. Ann and Adelia were sisters-in-law. Ann married Adelia's brother, William.[2] Besides those ties of marriage, Ann and Adelia had much in common and appear to have shared strong feelings for one another. Both of the women were born and raised in Natchez; both women were married to free men of color; both centered their lives around their households and their families; both knew the value of freedom; both were freed slaves. The women were only separated by distance.

The letters and other items the women exchanged were usually transported by Wellington West, a slave belonging to Adelia Johnson Miller and James Miller. Wellington regularly made the trip by boat between Natchez and New Orleans. He earned his living by transporting produce, seafood, cloth, and manufactured goods between the two ports. Evidence suggests that Wellington made a weekly trip between the two ports for decades and that he transported the family's goods and communications with him as he went. The convenience that his travels up and down the river offered the family was stopped temporarily on December 2, 1848, as Lavinia Miller wrote her Aunt Ann that "Welington's boat is sunk, but I got all my things you sent to me." Wellington eventually got another boat, and the family resumed their correspondence through him. Occasionally, other slaves would carry the letters and other goods the family exchanged. And on one occasion, William noted in his journal that he had sent Ann's letter to Adelia by the postal service. "Ann wrote to Mrs. Miller," he noted in his journal on July 24, 1837, "I paid the Postage on them both which I am affraid she wont Like so well." As William's remark and other evidence suggests, Ann struggled to keep the family finances under control.[3]

Wellington joined hundreds of other rivermen who worked the river between Natchez and New Orleans. The river provided the isolated ports and their residents with ties to the outside world. News in the form of letters, newspapers, and even gossip was carried by the many boats that traveled up and down the river. The river was the basis of commercial transportation. Barrels of salt, meat, apples, cornmeal, flour, and oats from the northern and western reaches of the river and its tributaries were transported downriver. Butter, shoes, and iron made their way down the river from New York; whiskey, mules, and hay from Kentucky; coal from Pittsburgh. Boats making their way upriver from New Orleans brought oysters, rice, spices, sugar, and molasses to the docks. The Crescent City served as the distribution center for the products transported upriver from around the world.

Natchez never enjoyed the commercial significance of New Orleans. Most of the year the boats that brought the goods to Natchez left with empty holds. It was only in the late summer that the boats left with their decks piled high with cotton. Between 1795 — the year that the cotton gin arrived in Natchez — and the eve of the Civil War, the Natchez region grew to typify the successes of the plantation South. Indeed, by that year the region's planters and slaves were producing more than four hundred thousand bales of cotton per year. That amounted to more than 10 percent of the cotton produced in the South. The agricultural success of the Natchez region depended upon the skill and labor of the region's planters and slaves. But another factor influenced the region's agricultural success and that was the river. Over the millennium that preceded the migration of planters and slaves into the region, the river had deposited a deep layer of rich, brown loam along its banks. It was that soil that served as the base for one of the most profitable crops in the plantation South. Anyone who doubted the region's agricultural successes simply had to watch the riverboats that called at the port during the early fall when cotton was picked and baled. Countless boats left the docks of the little port laden with thousand of bales of cotton. Cotton was packed in the holds of the boats, piled on their decks, and even strapped to their sides.[4]

Everyone in Natchez anxiously awaited the reports of the year's cotton crop. They knew that their fortunes were tied to the fleecy, white blossoms and to the river. Even though few Natchez merchants and artisans owned plantations, all were as dependent on the cotton crop as the planters and slaves of the hinterland. The townsfolk profited along with the local planters and farmers when the crop was abundant. They suffered losses when the crop declined. Thus, even though Ann and her family did not belong to the planter class but were instead a part of Natchez's merchant class, they, too, were as dependent on cotton production as their planter neighbors. And they too grew unusually wealthy as the little port, and the region around it, prospered.

The system of plantation agriculture that supported the city influenced far more than the port's economy. Slavery, the form of labor that prevailed in the South, ordered the structure of southern society, whether in the hinterlands or the entrepôts. The hierarchical nature of the South's social structure rested on the premise that slavery was defined by race. Africans or those of African descent, according to southern law and belief, were inferior and thus destined to be slaves. Whites, on the other hand, who were theoretically believed to be pure, were viewed as superior to blacks. Status, or social standing, was determined by one's position within the hierarchical social system. Race — and gender — were determinants of social status.

The place that a woman occupied in the social order was in principal determined by her skin color and heritage. White women were essential to the perpetuation of the slave system. They reproduced the slaveholding class. Because women were vessels through which property passed, their chastity and virtue were essential. Purity, chastity, and virtue were only ideals to which southern women should aspire, but, in principal, those conventions ordered the roles of women. Southern white women were submissive and dependent upon the protection and direction of their men.[5]

Slave women, on the other hand, were excluded from the ideals assigned to white women. Certainly, they were expected to be submissive and dependent. But even those traits detected within women of color were perceived differently than when found in the character of white women. Slave women were deemed impure and thus available for both debauching and breeding. They were expected to be completely submissive to their master, their mistress, or their overseer. They had no protection under the law. They had no rights. Their subordination, indeed, was determined in the law to be complete. But in the case of slave women, their domination was not only by owners or the owners' representatives but also by the men in their own families and communities.[6]

The free women of color represented in this volume were freed slaves or descendants of freed slaves. As a result, they were viewed by whites to be tainted by their ties to slavery and thus deemed to be incompatible with the ideals associated with white women. Yet despite their inability to meet the ideals of the ruling class, free women of color, by necessity, shaped their lives in response to those ideals. If they had not at least partially accepted such mores, free women of color would have brought disdain and degradation upon themselves and their families. For even though white men idealized the value of white women by assigning an identity to them that was denied to women of color, they also expected free women of color to at least aspire to the ideal. While these women shaped their identities in response to the dominant culture, they were also influenced by tradition within their own communities. Free women of color, like Ann Battles Johnson and Adelia Johnson Miller and their daughters, constructed a discreet identity that reflected neither that of black slave women nor of free white women. In response to their unique roles within southern society, they created instead another identity. It is that identity that the letters in this volume illustrate.

The women represented in this volume lived in a middle-class urban milieu. It was not unusual for free people of color to live in the South's entrepôts where they could draw upon family and friends to form their own communities. Some urban settings, such as New Orleans, Charleston, and Mobile, contained enough free people of color to support distinctive churches, schools, and social organizations. A small artisan class flourished in the ports along southern waterways, and it was not unusual for free men of color to dominate carpentry and masonry trades. They were also highly skilled metal workers and furniture craftsmen and often monopolized the cigar-making and barbering trades. Free women of color usually combined family and household responsibility with the necessity of work. Not every woman could depend on the financial support of men, and even if they could, few did. Therefore, the majority of free women of color extended their domestic world into that of the public. Free women of color were recognized as highly skilled laundresses, seamstresses, and cooks. Many of them inhabited the petty marketing trade within their communities.[7]

Free women of color participated to varying degrees in the market economy, whether married or not. Certainly Ann Battles Johnson continued to work after she was married. After three years of courtship, when she was twenty years old in April 1835, Ann married William Johnson. William was one of Natchez's most prosperous businessmen. Over the sixteen years of their marriage, between 1835 and 1851, Ann and William had nine children. Their first three children were sons. Their eldest, named for his father, was born in 1836. Their second, named Richard, was born in 1837; Byron was born in 1839. Their fourth child and first daughter was born March 25, 1841. They named her Ann after her mother but called her Anna. After the birth of her first daughter, Ann gave birth to seven more children. One, however, died in infancy, and another died in early childhood. Alice was born in 1842; Catharine in 1843; Phillip in 1844 (he died shortly after birth); Eugenia in 1845; Louis was born November 1846; Josephine in 1849. Ann's last child, Clarence, was born in 1851, just months before the death of her husband, William.[8]

Throughout the years of their marriage, Ann depended upon William to provide for her and for their growing family. By 1835, when he married Ann, William owned one barbershop; by 1850, he increased his holdings to three. His barbershops were the most successful in Natchez. He spend most of his days cutting hair, shaving faces, renting out the french baths that he had installed in his shops, and supervising his many apprentices. When William was not barbering, he was doing business with the local residents. He made small loans to his neighbors, making a profit through the interest he charged them. He also operated a small drayage company, and by 1845 he had purchased Hard Scrabble, a small cotton plantation south of the city. Despite the fact that he owned as many as eight slaves at one time, all his business activities created work that took him away from the house daily. Ann, on the other hand, stayed at home where she was in charge of the household.[9]

Ann's primary responsibilities were as a mother, a housekeeper, and a household manager. Throughout the early years of her marriage to William, Ann performed the household chores and cared for their children. Later, after the couple had become more prosperous, she employed slaves. It was that transition, the one that introduced slaves into the household, that transformed Ann from a housekeeper to a household manager. And it was also the addition of household slaves that enabled Ann to participate in the petty marketing trade of Natchez. Free women of color who lived in the Caribbean, Latin America, and the many entrepôts that were scattered across the South regularly sold goods in stalls or open air markets. Some even hawked their goods in the streets and alleyways of their neighborhoods. Others, like Ann, who either could or would choose to identify more closely with the middle-class image of the protected woman, owned slaves who did their selling for them. Records indicate that throughout the years that she owned slaves, Ann employed them to sell produce, baked goods, and dry goods.[10]

Several of the letters, Catharine's diary, and the household account books demonstrate that Ann and her daughters were accomplished seamstresses. They sewed for themselves and also produced garments and accessories that their slaves peddled. In her account book of March 1855, Ann noted that she had purchased 4 yards of linen and 20 yards of calico. On March 10, she purchased 10 yards of serge, 8 yards of the same, and 9 yards of black silk. On March 19, she bought 10 yards of serge, 3 yards of muslin, and 6 yards of calico. On March 22, she purchased 7 yards of calico; on the 23rd, 15 yards of calico, and 8 yards of calico. In April, she continued to purchase large quantities of fabric, as well as in July, September, and October.[11]

Other notations in an account book left by Ann demonstrate the success that her slaves had in selling the goods sewn by the women. During an unspecified period in March 1855, Ann's slave "Eliza sold 3 hoods, 2 bonnets, 2 small bonnets, 1 silk bonnet, 7 scarves, 4 spenser capes, 2 cravates, 5 caps, 2 head scarves, 3 rouches, head pins, and 1 headdress." In the same period, her slave Hannah sold "4 spencer capes, 4 scarves, 1 cravat, 2 caps, 6 pair mitts, 4 pair stockings, 2 bags, 3 old ladies caps." Evidence suggests that by working with her daughters and her slaves that Ann was able to successfully supplement her family's income.[12]

Ann's marketing business, however, did not provide her with the only source of income that she used to run her household. Throughout all the years of her marriage, Ann received a household allowance from William. For most of the years, she received one dollar a day. But in 1849, William must have decided that Ann did not need as much of a household allowance for the sum was reduced to fifty cents. Ann used the household allowance that William allotted to her to purchase supplies for the household. Other evidence in the account books demonstrates that William purchased a few products in bulk in places where Ann would not have gone. For instance, on the 29th of July 1836, William purchased four barrels of flour for $4.12. He purchased three barrels of coal on December 2, 1836, and forty more barrels on December 5. Other than that, William purchased barrels of sugar and sacks of coffee, cornmeal, and rice.[13]

But neither Ann nor William purchased all the goods and produce that they needed for their household. Instead, Ann produced much of what they needed in the small space of their backyard. There she kept a garden where she grew squash, turnips, okra, peas, beans, and tomatoes. She also had a chicken coop and a pig pen. Her cows, pigs, turkeys, and chickens provided her family with meat; the chickens gave the family eggs. These things were not all that she produced. She also kept a cow and horses across the street from the house. The cow supplied the family with milk. Ann provided her family with the produce and meat, but she also sold what her family did not consume.[14]

The money Ann earned contributed to the general wealth and social standing of her family, and it eventually helped to finance her children's education. Because Ann's children were not welcome in the racially biased community of Natchez, they received their education at home from their mother and father. They were tutored in reading and writing, mathematics, literature, and geography. The boys, it appears, were trained additionally by their father to become businessmen and barbers. The girls were also instructed in music, and their mother taught them sewing and other domestic skills. The children's home schooling was supplemented by hired tutors. And later, at least William, Richard, Byron, and Anna were sent to school in New Orleans, where several schools educated the children of free people of color.[15]

Ann not only worked to provide for her family but also exchanged goods with Adelia Johnson Miller and her daughters in New Orleans. Because the port of New Orleans was so close to the Gulf and the lakes, bays, and bayous of south Louisiana, the Miller's had access to oysters, fish, and other seafood. The markets in New Orleans also stocked lemons, limes, and other more tropical produce that would have been difficult or expensive for the women in Natchez to obtain. Therefore, instead of doing without, or paying exorbitant fees for goods and produce, by working together the women could exchange supplies with each other. On February 16, 1844, Adelia wrote to her brother to tell him that "the pig that mother sent me was so fine that Miller invited two or three of his friends to dine with him and so I had to prepare dinner for them. It was really a fine pig and you will please tell mother that I thank her a thousand times for it. Tell her that her health was drank and the health of all her boys also." A few years later Octavia, Adelia's daughter and Ann's niece, wrote Ann in what was probably December 1849: "Deare Aunt, I have done the best I could in getting your things that you bid me to get. I got you three Dimes Worth of nutmeg and all so two dimes Worth of cinnamon that is the best that I could Aunt and, I hope that it Will please you fore I did do the best I could." While some goods were more plentiful and thus cheaper in New Orleans, others were easier to obtain in Natchez. Adelia wrote Ann in October 1847 to "[a]sk Mother to try and get me some eggs if she can and send them down by this boat. They are four [bits] a doz here and not good at that." Ann also sent nuts, turkeys, and a variety of produce from her garden to New Orleans.[16]

Both Ann and Adelia took their ability to freely participate in the markets of their cities seriously. They also enjoyed their ability to participate in an exchange network between the ports and they especially enjoyed the diversity and maneuverability they had in their everyday lives. Neither of the women took their freedom for granted as both had been born to mothers who were slaves. Harriett Battles and Amy Johnson had been slaves when they bore their children, and because the condition of the child followed that of the mother, their children were legally defined as slaves. Thus both Ann Battles and William and Adelia Johnson were born as slaves. Furthermore, none were emancipated until they were adults, or nearly adults. James Miller, Adelia's husband, was born free in Philadelphia before he moved south to Natchez, where he met and married Adelia.[17]

Freedom had not come easily to Ann or to any of her family members. By the 1820s, the laws for manumission in Mississippi had become extremely restrictive. The slave codes in Mississippi had never been lenient, but in 1822 the Mississippi legislature passed a law that sought to preserve slavery and to prevent manumission. According to the law, slaves could be manumitted only if the master could prove that the slave had committed a meritorious act for the owner or for the state. A special act of the legislature was required for each manumission. Only six petitions for manumission were introduced to the legislature in 1823. Just three were approved. Masters and mistresses were forced to look elsewhere for the freedom of their slaves.[18]

Some simply let their slaves go free, but that was risky. Slaves who passed illegally into freedom might be identified as illegally free and reenslaved. Other Mississippians had their slaves freed in Louisiana and then returned them to the state, even though that too violated Mississippi's law. Ann's mother, Harriett, and William's and Adelia's mother, Amy, were taken to Louisiana and freed. Louisiana had always had the most liberal manumission policies of any of the southern colonies or states. A demographic imbalance had persisted during Louisiana's colonial period, prompting a preponderance of interracial liaisons. Slaveholders and their neighbors regularly turned to slave women for companionship, and many of the women, recognizing the benefits of such a relationship for themselves and for their children, responded. Even though such liaisons were frowned on, they were generally tolerated and many grew to resemble de facto marriages. Unlike British-American slaveholders to the north, some slaveholders and cohabitants took pride in freeing their de facto wives along with their racially mixed children. Thousands of such manumissions occurred in Louisiana where a large population of racially mixed free persons of color evolved into a community. It was only in Louisiana that such racially mixed people were presumed to be free. That presumption remained extremely significant to free people of color and to slaves who hoped to gain their freedom.[19]

Amy Johnson had been the first member of the large extended Johnson-Miller family to be emancipated. The process of her freedom was begun on March 20, 1814, when her master, the white William Johnson, who was more than likely the father of her racially mixed son and daughter, William and Adelia, took her across the river to Vidalia, Louisiana, where he petitioned the court to free her. At that time, according to Louisiana law, the white William Johnson had to testify that Amy was able to support herself, that for the past four years she had been honest, and that she had not attempted to escape or commit any crime. He obligated himself to maintain her should she "be in want oweing to sickness, old age, insanity, or any other proven infirmity." After the court hearing, a notice of manumission for Amy was posted on the courthouse door so that "every person who may have any legal opposition to said Emancipation are required to file said opposition in the Office of the Parish Court of said Parish, within forty days from the date of the present." Evidently no one objected to her manumission because Amy was declared legally free forty days later in May 1814.[20]

Ann's mother, Harriett, was freed in much the same manner as Amy. The process of Harriett's freedom was begun in June 1822 when she too was taken by her master, Gabriel Tichenor, to Vidalia, Louisiana, where he petitioned the court to free her. The notice of the pending manumission of Harriett was posted on the courthouse door so that anyone with a legal opposition had forty days to object. No one objected to Harriett's manumission either because it was granted on June 25, 1822.[21]

Neither Harriett's child, Ann, nor Amy's children, William and Adelia, were freed with their mothers. Laws in Louisiana accommodated the manumission of Amy and Harriett. But those same laws, in effect between 1807 and 1827, specifically forbid the manumission of slaves under the age of thirty. Gabriel Tichenor was not willing to wait until Ann was thirty years old. Instead, in 1826, four years after freeing Harriett, Tichenor traveled with Harriett and her daughter to Cincinnati where he petitioned for Ann's freedom and re-petitioned for that of Harriett. According to the petition, Tichenor requested that Harriett, who was described as "a mulatress aged about 34 and her child named Ann about 11 years old" be freed in consideration for Harriett's faithful service. The freedom of Harriett and Ann was granted by the authorities of Ohio on April 27, 1826.[22]

Like Ann, Adelia and William remained in slavery after their mother was freed. They, like Ann, were too young to be freed under Louisiana law. Therefore, in 1818, four years after emancipating Amy, the white William Johnson freed Amy's daughter, Adelia, who was thirteen years old. In order to insure her freedom he chose to send her to Philadelphia with a designated agent, George Ralston of Natchez. Then two years later, on January 21, 1820, William Johnson petitioned the state legislature, in session in Natchez, to free Amy's child William. He wrote in his petition that Amy had been freed as a result of her good conduct but that William had been prevented from freedom by his minority and incapacity to execute a bond. The elder William certified that he was a resident of the state of Mississippi and that he had no outstanding debts to prevent the manumission. He then testified that manumitting the slave boy would give "liberty to a human being which all are entitled to as a Birthright, & extend the hand of humanity to a rational Creature, on whom unfortunately Complexion, Custom & even law in this land of freedom, has conspired to rivet the fetters of freedom." The next day after being presented to the lower house, the petition was referred to a special committee that wrote a bill providing for William's emancipation. It was amended and then finally passed by both houses on Febrary 10, 1820.[23]

Freedom for slaves in Natchez, or anywhere else in Mississippi, was rare, so the few who obtained it never took it for granted. White Mississippians, like whites across the South, had always restricted the activities of slaves and free people of color. But beginning in the 1820s, the free people of color in Mississippi faced increasingly restrictive laws and attitudes. The laws put in place to restrict the growth of the freed population were put in place in the 1820s, but they did not work as effectively as the state's slaveholders and legislators hoped. The number of free people of color in the territory in 1800 only numbered 182. By 1810, the free-colored population had grown to 240, a 32 percent increase. By 1820, there were 458 free people of color in the state; that number amounted to a 91 percent increase. The rate of growth had declined but the absolute numbers increased between 1820 and 1830. In 1830, the population had increased to 519 — a 13 percent increase. In 1840 the population experienced its greatest increase. In that year the population grew to 1,366, a number that represented a 163 percent increase. By 1850, the population suffered a severe decline, not only in the rate of growth but also in the actual numbers. In that year, the population of free people of color had dropped to 913; that amounted to a 33 percent decline. By 1860, the population had declined again to 773, a 15.5 percent decline.[24]

Ann and her family only had to look around to see how rare and privileged their status was. Many of Mississippi's counties did not have even one free person of color as a resident. The counties that contained the majority of the population of free people of color were the four southwest counties on the Mississippi River that were originally settled by the French and Spanish. More than one-half of the free population could be found in that region of the state. Adams County, which included Natchez, was one of those counties. In 1840 there were more than 283 free people of color there, and of those, 207 lived in Natchez. By 1850, that segment of the population of Adams County had declined to 258. Only forty-five people of color who lived in Adams County lived outside of Natchez.[25]

The state's slaveholders and legislators had never been satisfied with just stemming the growth of the free population. Slaveholders in Mississippi, as elsewhere across the South, had actively sought to turn the tide of opposition to slavery that had accompanied the American Revolution. One of the primary ways in which they sought to strengthen their positions as slaveholders was to exchange their argument that slavery was a necessary evil for the other argument that held that slavery was a positive good. According to the "necessary evil" argument, human bondage was an evil institution that slaveholders had inherited from their ancestors. It was not an institution of their making, but one that they were committed to uphold. That argument, that slavery was a necessary evil, however, was replaced during the 1830s by one that held that slavery was a positive good. "Negroes were by nature an inferior race of beings," argued William Laughton Smith, a South Carolina Congressman; they needed the care and support of whites. Because slaves were naturally inferior and required care by their owners, the rationale continued, free people of color were a destablizing and undesirable element of the population and should not be tolerated.[26]

The shift to the stance that not only was slavery a positive good but also that free people of color were dangerous was reinforced by the Nat Turner Rebellion of 1831. Even though free people of color had little to do with that or with any other rebellion, whites directed their ire at that hapless segment of the population. The racial assaults were harsh in Mississippi where the white residents of the state moved rapidly to restrict, if not reverse, the growth of the free-colored population. White residents of the river counties, led by people in Natchez, especially feared the free people of color who they believed represented a real threat to the social order. In particular, it was pointed out that a substantial segment of the free-colored population of the river towns had immigrated into the state in express violation of the law. By the 1830s, the only way in which the population of Mississippi could increase legally was through natural increase or the manumission of slaves through specific acts of the legislature. A few people illegally migrated into the state. Occasionally slaves were taken out of the state, manumitted, and then returned, as Ann, Harriett, Amy, and Adelia had been.[27]

An editor of a local newspaper the *Natchez* captured the changing attitude of the white community when he wrote on March 5, 1831, that "if the free coloured people were removed, the slaves could safely be treated with more indulgence. Less fear would be entertained, and greater lattitude of course allowed. . . . In a word, it would make better masters and better slaves. From the same cause also results another evil: the check or rather stop, which has been given to the emancipation of slaves, no matter how meritorious their conduct."[28] In one of its most restrictive policies, the Mississippi legislature moved in that year to require free people of color to leave the state within a stipulated period of time. Free people who were in "good standing" were allowed to offer petitions containing the signatures of reputable white men to the county board of police in order to remain in the state. The most perceivable influence the increasing restrictiveness had on the Johnson-Miller family was in 1830 when James Miller decided to take Adelia and their children and move to New Orleans where racial attitudes and laws were less threatening.

The status of free people of color in Mississippi continued to be severely restricted. By 1840, laws had been passed that expressly prohibited them from testifying against whites, voting, holding office, serving in the militia, or violating the unwritten social code of the community. Neither the restrictions nor the changing attitudes seem to have radically affected Ann or her family during the 1830s. It was during that decade that Ann and William married and established themselves and their family in the community. They had begun to question their safety, however, by the summer of 1841 when a campaign was launched against Natchez's free people of color.

On August 7 of that year, William wrote in his journal: "Large meeting was Intended to have been held in the City Hall tho I understand there was not a greate many thare." The explanation of the meeting is found in an announcement in the Natchez *Courier,* which was placed there by several concerned "citizens." The announcement read:

> *FREE NEGROES AND SLAVES.* A general meeting of the citizens of Adams County is requested at the Court House in Natchez at 5 O'Clock in the afternoon of Saturday next, the 7th instant, to take into consideration the propriety of enforcing the 26th section of the Revised code of the laws of Mississippi, imposing a fine of the owners of slaves who permit them to go at large and hire their time; and also of enforcing the 80th section of the same code, requiring free persons of color to remove from the State and to prevent their emigration into the state.[29]

Despite the small turnout, the group organized itself into a vigilance committee in order to investigate and deport any free people of color who might be accused of violating the law. In that month the vigilance committee began to arrest free people of color in order to put them on trial. At stake was whether the arrested could remain in Natchez. In just one example of the near hysteria that gripped the town in August 1841, a resident wrote a letter on August 17 to the Natchez *Free Trader,* another local newspaper, urging his neighbors to act promptly "to strike a severe blow against the practices of the rogue, the incendiary, and the abolitionist" by regulating slave conduct and by "the immediate removal of every free negro, who has intruded upon our society."[30] On the same day, William wrote in his journal that "all sorts of Tryals going on — The different offices have been full all day and they continue to arrest Still — The Lord knows who those things will terminate for I have no conception myself."

On August 18 he wrote that "[t]he Horrows [horrors] of the Inquisition is going On still in this City, It Seems that Dr. Merrill and the Jg [Judge] has a tryal this Evening. I have not herd any moore about it. The report of Harriet Cullen or Harriet Johnson being in Jail is not true, She was not put in Jail, Glad of it." [31]

Even though free people of color who remained in the state were required by law to obtain a petition containing the signatures of respected white men, neither Ann nor William were required to present such a petition. Evidently, the family's social standing spoke for itself. But the family did experience the degradation of the law when William was forced to secure petitions for his free colored apprentices. He described the irony of the situation when he commented on the men who signed the petitions. "Those names are an Ornament to Any paper — Those are Gentlemen of the 1st Order of Talents and Standing." To the horror of Ann and William several of their acquaintances were deported from the state. William wrote in his journal on September 5, 1841, that "some of the free people of color were ordered off. For instance Dembo and maryan Gibson. They are as far as I know inocent and harmless People. And have never done a Crime. . . . Oh what a Country we Live in." [32]

Even though Ann and William had become prosperous and respected members of their community by the 1840s, they had grown increasingly concerned about their safety and the safety of their children. Their status was threatened every time an acquaintance was arrested and tried. Their safety was threatened every time someone was deported from the state. Ann must have felt particularly threatened by steps being taken to deport free people of color who had been illegally freed and that included her, as she had been taken out of the state, freed, and then returned. Ann would have been concerned that if the Natchez vigilance committee decided to arrest her and put her on trial, she and perhaps her children could be deported, or even worse, reenslaved. It was probably that threat that compelled Ann in the summer of 1842 to take extraordinary steps to ensure the safety of her children by traveling to New Orleans.

It was highly unusual for Ann to travel. Over her lifetime, it appears that she rarely left Natchez. The first time she left was when she traveled to Cincinnati in order to obtain her freedom. Her only other trips appear to have been to New Orleans. The first trip that Ann made to New Orleans was in July 1842, the trip was especially difficult for her. The only overland route from Natchez to New Orleans was along the Natchez Trace, but even the flatboatmen who had brought their crops down the Mississippi avoided the Trace. Cutthroats and criminals waited along the overland route for travelers they could rob. Travel by steamboat was much safer for Ann, but even then, her trip would be no simple journey for her because her social position as a respected, prosperous, racially mixed free woman of color complicated matters.[33]

Because William made the arrangements for Ann's trip he commented on the transaction in his journal. In the entry dated July 9, 1842, he wrote

> I spoke to A. L. Willson the other day to procure me a passage on the Steam Boat, Maid of Arkensaw, which he promised to do and to day when the Boat Came I went down to see about it and I saw him and He told me that he had spoke to the Capt. and that he had refuse to Let a State Room, But that my wife Could have the whole of the Ladies Cabbin to Herself but it was a Rule of his Boat not to Let any Col persons have State Room on Her — I asked him to go with me on Bourd — He went on Board and showd me the Capt. and I asked him if I could not spare a State Room and he told me that He Could not spare one that it was against the Rules of His Boat and that he had said it once and that was Enough and that he was a man of his word and Spoke of Prejudice of the Southern people, it was damd Foolish &c, and that he was a doing a Business for other people and was Compelld to adopt those Rules — I did not prevail by no means — He then said that I Could Have a State Room on Conditions which I told him would answer.[34]

William's terse report of his conversation with the captain does not reveal the conditions that "would answer." He only noted in his entry of July 10 that his family had "left for New Orleans yesterday — I was alone to day to dinner."[35] But what is clear is that he risked a great deal by stepping over the established boundaries that guided his interaction with whites by insisting on a stateroom for Ann and their children. Mississippi, like other southern states, had laws that forbid free men of color from insulting whites. These laws imposed a terrible pressure on free people of color who were forced to watch every public word and deed and even then could be jailed, publicly punished, or forced to leave town by a disgruntled white. His action was unusual, for the records suggest that neither William nor Ann openly challenged the social conventions of the world around them. Instead, they struggled to fit into that world, even as they rejected many of its conditions and implications.

But why, one must wonder, did William insist on the stateroom for Ann? Perhaps J. S. Buckingham, a traveler and commentator of southern life, offers an explanation when he described the humiliation heaped on free women of color who were traveling aboard the steamboat *Jefferson*. "Among the passengers in the ladies' cabin," Buckingham wrote in his travel journal, "were three coloured females, going from Mobile to Montgomery, whose position was very remarkable." The women, Buckingham noted, were "not negresses, but mulattoes of dark-brown colour and strongly marked African features, and appeared to be sisters or relatives. They were each dressed much more expensively than either of the white ladies on board — silks, lace, and feathers, white ornaments of jewelry of various kinds, being worn by them." Then Buckingham described the disgrace directed at the women who were forced to sleep on the cabin floor, "as the coloured servants usually do, no berth or bed-place being assigned to them." The next morning, however, as Buckingham pointed out, the women "occupied a good hour at their toilette, with the white stewardess." After finishing their toilette, Buckingham wrote the women "remained sitting in cabin all day, as if they were on a footing of perfect equality with the white passengers; but when mealtime came, then was seen the difference."

Buckingham recognized the contradictions that the social conventions of race and gender imposed upon free women of color, and he correctly acknowledged the contradictions that defined the social positions of the women. As Buckingham suggests, there was no place for free women of color in the hierarchically stratified social system of the South. In his description of the anomalous status of free women of color he had observed, Buckingham relied on the dining arrangements on the *Jefferson* to personify the stratification so necessary for the perpetuation of this social order and the trouble that those in authority took to reinforce it. "The order in which the meals were taken in the steam-vessel," according to Buckingham, "was this: at the first bell, the captain and all the white passengers sat down; when these had finished and left the table, a second bell summoned the pilot, the captain's clerk, all the white men of the engineer's department, the white stewardess, and such white servants or subordinates as might be on board; and when these had finished, the third bell summoned the black steward and all the mulattoes and coloured servants, to take their meal."

Buckingham wrote, however, that

so equivocal . . . was the position of these coloured ladies, that they could not be placed at either of the tables; they were not high enough in rank to be seated with the whites, and they were too high to be seated with the blacks and mulattoes; so they had to retire to the pantry, where they took their meals standing; and the contrast of their finery in dress and ornament, with the place in which they took their isolated and separate meal, was painfully striking. What rendered it more so, to me at least, was this — that however a man might yearn to break down those barriers which custom and prejudice has raised against a certain race, the exhibition of any such feeling, or the utterance of any such sentiment, would undoubtedly injure the very parties for whom his sympathy might be excited, or on whose behalf it might be expressed.[36]

William recognized the degradation that Ann would have suffered had she traveled in the ladies' cabin. Instead, he knew that if she had a stateroom and was secluded from contact with whites, she could avoid the typical degredation aimed at free women of color. The trip from Natchez to New Orleans took about one and a half days, depending on the speed of the boat and the number of port calls the boat made. If the boat did not stop the trip could take a little more than a day, but if it called at Baton Rouge, for instance, the trip could take a day and a half to two days. William knew that either way, Ann could be subjected to sleeping on the floor and taking her meals standing in the galley. And too, Ann was not traveling alone. She took her children with her: William, six years old; Richard, four; Byron, three; Anna, one and a half. Alice, who was only three months old, stayed at home with her father and a slave. Ann was accompanied by her mother and a slave.[37]

After arriving in New Orleans, Ann more than likely stayed with Adelia, James, and their children. She also visited with friends and acquaintances who lived there. And no doubt she spent some of her time in the city, stocking up on staples and produce not available in the small port of Natchez. But that was not why Ann made the difficult trip with her family. A far more pressing need compelled her to travel to New Orleans — it was during that trip that she had her children baptized at St. Louis Cathedral.[38] But why did Ann feel the need to take her children all the way to New Orleans in the heat of the summer amidst the fear of yellow fever to have them baptized? Why not have them baptized in the Catholic church in Natchez? The answers to the questions are not simple, for it appears that her motivation was as much political as it was religious.

The Catholic church in Louisiana, as epitomized by the St. Louis Cathedral in New Orleans, had always been especially concerned with the well-being of the free people of color. Missionaries accompanied the French into the colony, and the church encouraged slaveholders to ameliorate conditions for their slaves. When the Spanish began to govern the region after 1769, free people of color began to forge a central place in the hierarchy of the church. Their place developed as a consequence of the unique political conditions within Spanish governance. During that period, which lasted from 1769 to 1803, the Spanish clergy antagonized the already hostile French planters who reacted by withdrawing much of their support from secular and religious officials. Recognizing that in its concern for the salvation of their souls, the church would be a powerful ally, and the free people of color were soon filling the place deserted by the French. A survey made of the records of the St. Louis Cathedral in New Orleans demonstrates that of the 724 children and adults baptized there in 1800, 69 percent were slaves and free people of color. When counted together, slaves and free people of color only totaled approximately 54 percent of the population in 1800, and the majority of those reported to have regularly attended the cathedral were free people of color. In general, it was the church that acted to protect the free people of color. And it was the church that protected them individually. For it was within the church records that their identities were faithfully recorded and preserved as free.[39]

Thus it was to the church in New Orleans that Ann took her children to be baptized. William was baptized at the cathedral March 31, 1842. Byron, Richard, and Anna were baptized on July 23, 1842. They were eligible for baptism in Louisiana because their mother told the priest that they had been born in Concordia Parish. Once baptized and recorded as such in the sacramental books as free by the priest in New Orleans, the status of Ann's children as free was secured. Ann returned to St. Louis Cathedral in 1848 to have Louis baptized. Then she returned once more on June 13, 1856. On that date, she had Alice, Catharine, Eugenia, Josephine, and Clarence baptized. Their identities as free people of color were officially recorded and protected.[40]

While Ann was able to do something about the safety of the status of her children, she could do little about their health and the health of her other family members. Letters written to Ann always began with news of the well-being of the writers and their families. The inhabitants of the Gulf Coast were subject to many deadly diseases, such as whooping cough, tuberculosis, pneumonia, and measles, and the women worried constantly over the effects such diseases could have on their children. When Adelia wrote to Ann in October 1847 she began with the standard salutation: "I write you these few lines to inform you that we are all well at present esccept Little verania and she is still down with that foot. And I am glad to hear that you are injoying your healths." [41]

Besides the health risks of any population in the nineteenth century, the inhabitants of the Gulf Coast were repeatedly subjected to severe epidemics of yellow fever. In a letter dated May 20, 1855, Emma Hoggatt wrote to her Aunt Ann that "there is so much sickness here now the people is just dropping like flies, especially children." But Emma had a special reason to worry. She continued, "I thought I would of lost my baby thursday morning he was taking with such a sever cramp cholic. He just turned as pale as death and was screaming all the time just as if some one was sticking pins in him. . . ." Besides her worry for her family members, Emma closed her letter with news of the deaths of four mutual acquaintances. [42]

As these letters demonstrate, women were more likely to have complications with their health than men. After all, women not only had to survive the general illnesses of the day, but also the complications associated with childbirth. When Emma wrote to her Aunt Ann of her fear for her son, she was recuperating from an abscessed breast that had nearly taken her life. Shortly after the birth of her son the preceding March, Emma had written to her aunt, "I have just lain for days and nights and did nothing else but cried. . . ." Like other women, Emma lived in fear for her life and for that of her infant. But even while Emma worried over her son, she also delighted in his precociousness. In the same letter in which she wrote of her debilitating and excruciating pain, she proudly wrote "as to my baby he's just the finest boy you ever looked at. He takes so much notice all of everything. He laughs all ready and trys his best to crow when you talk to him." As so lovingly expressed in the sentiments in this letter, concern for their children preoccupied these women. [43]

No matter how much care they took, however, the women did not always survive to care for their offspring. On January 9, 1848, William wrote in his journal that a friend Louis Wiley had come from New Orleans on that day and that he said that "Mrs. Miller (Adelia) is very low indeed and that I aught to go down and see her as soon as Possible." He wrote the next day on January 10 that he had "got off for N. Orleans this day on S.B. Rio grand." He wrote the next day that he was on the river in the morning but arrived about four or five o'clock and

Started to the Residence of Mr Miller where I Exspected to find My Poor Dear Sister alive, but on geting near the House Patsy [one of the Miller's slaves] told me that she was Dead. Oh, Mercifull Father, Have Mercy on me — Oh my Greate God. When I Got to the House and Saw in all its Rooms no trace of my Poor Much Loved Sister. She was Burried on yesterday — Oh merciful Father Have Mercy on me, and Grant oh Mercifull God that She is Happy — How Glad I am Oh God that I hear that she said that she was Prepared to die and that she felt resigned to Leave this world.

Adelia had died of tuberculosis on January 8, 1848.[44]

Adelia was only forty-two years old when she died, but she had come to know death intimately before her own. Adelia, like so many other southern women, had lost a child. Her infant daughter, Catharine, had died January 17, 1842, as an infant. Adelia's death, in January 1848, however, spared her the knowledge of the premature death of another of her children. Just six weeks after her death, Adelia's sixteen-year-old son, James, died.[45]

Tragedy visited the Johnson branch of the family in 1844 when William and Ann lost their infant son Phillip and again in 1848 when their child Louis died. Death called once again in 1851 with the murder of Ann's husband, William. Perhaps it is not fair to say that nothing could have been more devastating to the family than William's death, but that is what leaps off the pages of the family papers. The devastation wrought by William's death was not just a result of the personal loss the family experienced. That fundamental loss was exaggerated by the manner in which William died — he was senselessly murdered in an act of violence that left the family stunned and isolated.

Events that led to William's death can be traced to 1845. It was during that summer that he sought to improve his financial and social standing by purchasing a 120-acre farm called Hard Scrabble. A few months later William added another 242 acres to this property when he bought out William Mosbey, the farmer next door. Hard Scrabble was located about seven miles southwest of Natchez on the banks of the Mississippi River. The property that comprised Hard Scrabble bordered the meandering Mississippi River except for one boundary. That boundary, which ran through a swamp, eventually became a point of contention between William and his neighbor, Baylor Wynn.

All had been quiet at Hard Scrabble until 1849 when Wynn purchased the adjacent property and began to cut timber without regard to the boundary line. William tried for two years to work out his differences with Wynn over the property line. He first simply demanded that Baylor Wynn cease cutting timber on his property. Failing that, he obtained two surveys in order to establish the exact position of his property line. Finally, he decided to take the matter to court. But in May 1851, just before his case was to be heard, William proposed a compromise, which was accepted. Everyone believed that the case had been amicably settled. A month later, however, on June 16, 1851, William decided to ride out to the farm with one of his sons, a slave, and one of his young apprentices Edward Hoggatt. That evening, as William and his party left the farm to return to Natchez, he was shot and fatally wounded. In a brief moment of coherence in the middle of the night, just before he died, William named Baylor Wynn as his assassin.

The assassination was described the next day in an article published in the Natchez *Courier*.

Our city on Tuesday morning, by hearing that what could only be deemed a horrible and deliberate murder had been committed upon an excellent and most inoffensive man. It was ascertained that William Johnson, a free man of color, born and raised in Natchez, and holding a respected position on account of his character, intelligence and deportment, had been shot, together with a young mulatto boy, about three miles below town, as they were returning home just before sunset on Monday evening last, in company with a son of Johnson and one of his negro slaves. From the testimony elicited before the Coroner's Jury, we learn the following facts. The party had been down the river a few miles, and in returning had stopped for Johnson to light a segar, at the house of a young man named Wynn, with those father (Baylor Wynn) Johnson had had a legal dispute relative to the boundary of their plantations, which adjoined each other. The dispute had been decided in favor of Johnson, who for the sake of peace had dismissed the suit, settling it at less than his legal rights. While sitting upon their horses near this house, Baylor Wynn entered. Having lighted his segar, Johnson with his party rode off. About three or four miles from this place they were much astonished to see Wynn riding near them, and leaving the road to go into the bushes. Shortly after, Johnson saw him again in another direction going behind some bushes a short distance from the road. A few minutes after a gun was fired from the bushes, three buckshot therefrom striking Johnson, one entering his lungs and going through him, one passing through him along the lower part of his back and one going through his arm. His horse was also wounded. The mulatto boy with him was also badly wounded by a shot entering his back, and lodging under the skin immediately over the abdomen. Johnson fell from his horse within a few yards from where he was struck, while the mulatto boy had strength enough, wounded as he was, to ride to town after assistance. Johnson died at two o'clock, that night. His dying declarations were taken in form, charging upon Baylor Wynn the commission of the crime. The boy still lies in great danger, and it is doubtful whether he can recover.

Wynn was arrested that same night and committed to jail. Very strong circumstancial testimony points to him as guilty of the deed. The tracks of the horse where he went behind the bushes were all measured, and identified beyond question, as those of Wynn's horse. His negro slaves declare that shortly after sunset he came in riding that horse, and ordered it rubbed down and taken care of. He had previously been repeatedly heard to threaten Johnson's life, and to say that the settlement of the suit was not the end of their difficulty. The Coroner's Jury which sat on Tuesday morning returned a verdict that Johnson came to his death by a wound or wounds inflicted by Baylor Wynn. Wynn is to be brought up for examination on Saturday (tomorrow) morning, when the whole case will be thoroughly investigated. Wynn, we understand, claims to be a white man, and has voted and given testimony as such. On this point will depend the admissibility of much of the testimony against him. This murder has created a great deal of excitement, as well from its atrocity, as from the peaceable character of Johnson and his excellent standing. His funeral services were conducted by the Rev. Mr. Watkins, who paid a just tribute to his memory, holding up his example as one well worthy of imitation by all of his class. We observed very many of the most respected citizens at his funeral. Johnson left a wife, nine children, and quite a handsome property; probably twenty to thirty thousand dollars.[46]

Baylor Wynn was held in jail for two years. He was tried three times. But despite its best effort, the state was never able to convict him. Instead, in an ironic twist of fate, Baylor Wynn, who was known by many in the community as a free man of color, escaped conviction by claiming to be a white man. Wynn's defense was successful because Mississippi law forbid any person who was black or racially mixed from testifying against any white. William Johnson's son, his slave, and his apprentice were all either black or racially mixed. The family was bitterly disappointed at each verdict. William Jr., Ann's oldest son, wrote to her in May 1853 just before Wynn's final trial took place in Woodville, Mississippi. In his letter he wrote, "You wrote me word that the excitement was rising again about the trial, as the time was drawing near. I hope the excitement ain't died away on our side and I trust to god he wont get clear." But Baylor Wynn did get clear, even though the family had obtained documents from King William County, Virginia, that traced the Wynn family back to 1802 confirming that they were free people of color. A ruling by the judge, however, kept the documents from being placed in evidence.[47]

William's sudden death in 1851 left Ann to assume responsibility for her large family, a duty she shouldered until her own death in 1866. At the time of William's death, he and Ann were among the most wealthy free people of color in Mississippi. A conservative estimate demonstrates that the Natchez *Courier* was correct in its estimate of the family worth. The Johnson's had accumulated property in excess of $25,000. That figure included slaves valued at $6,000, land at nearly $8,000, farm tools and stock at $1,600, and two houses on Main Street at $7,500.[48]

After their husband's death, most women would have depended upon an advisor, either a family member or a friend for financial guidance, but there is no evidence that Ann did either. Instead, it appears that she managed the family's finances entirely on her own, even making decisions that William would have more than likely disapproved. William failed to earn a significant profit from either Hard Scrabble or his other farm properties, and Ann had not been involved previously with the administering of the family's farm properties. In a move that separated her financial strategy from that of William's, in 1853 Ann sold all the farm property and property leases. She sold the family's rural property to James Surget for $7,812.50, for a profit of $3,612.50 over the $4,200.00 William had paid for it. William might not have made much of a profit on the property, but Ann did.[49]

Like many other middle-class urban dwellers in the South, the Johnson's had made it a practice to rent out rooms in their home. Later, after the family began to accumulate enough capital to invest, they purchased additional buildings and leased them. Ann continued the practice of leasing out rooms and buildings in order to supplement the family income after William's death. One of the receipts in the family papers, for instance, reveals that shortly after William's death she leased a room to Mr. Carter for the sum of fifty dollars. Leasing unimproved land, rooms in private homes and boarding houses, entire houses, and space for businesses was routine practice in the urban southern setting.[50]

Besides leasing out the bottom floor of her house, Ann also managed the barbershops William left, hiring barbers and looking to her sons to run the business there. Ann, however, was not satisfied to just manage the property left behind by William. She built another building on a piece of property owned by the family on Main Street, which she also leased out. Ann was fortunate to have income produced by her property; however it was unreliable. Tenants came and went. Some of the property apparently went unleased for long periods of time. Even when properties were rented, many tenants failed to meet the terms of their leases. Besides that Ann was faced with contant upkeep on the buildings, which receipts demonstrate were always in need of repairs.[51]

Ann made one other significant financial change after William's death. Beginning in 1854, she constructed a brick building on the family lot on Main Street in which William, Richard, and Byron continued the barbering business they had learned from their father. Only Clarence, Ann's youngest son, chose a career path other than barbering. But then, after all, Clarence was an infant when his father was murdered, and he did not enjoy his guidance as had his older brothers; Clarence chose to become a black-smith. During this time, Ann's daughters continued to work under their mother's tutorage, learning skills from her that she, in turn, had learned from her mother. Under Ann's direction, the day-to-day rhythm of family life continued much the same as it had before William's death. Indeed, it appears that until the Civil War, the family's prosperity, their household and slaves, their work rhythms, and the education of the children continued uninterrupted.[52]

Ann pursued other means of income. By the late 1850s, she was making business loans to her acquaintances in Natchez. She wrote in her account book on Tuesday, January 4, 1856, that she had loaned Aunt Hester Cumings $50. She noted on January 9, 1856, that she had sent $1,200 to Dr. Duncan "to put out at interest," or invest, for her. She added, "I hope i will have good luck with it."[53]

It was only with the war that Ann's income declined. There were few letters between Ann and her family and friends in New Orleans during the Civil War years and their aftermath. What those years held for the family is better understood through the sporadic pages of Catharine's diary.

Catharine, the sixth child and third daughter of Ann Battles Johnson and William Johnson, began keeping a diary in 1864 when she was twenty-two years old. The diary reproduced here appears to be the first and only one she kept. In her second entry dated May 1864, she wrote, "I have not written any since Tuesday the 10. How Lazy. I shall never make a good Chronicleir." Perhaps Catharine kept her diary as a way to remember her father. He had kept a journal throughout his adult life. She writes of her childhood before his death and the darkness after. "My mind goes back to the past with its Joys and sorrows," she wrote. "Back to the time when we were *happy thoughtless children* when the earth seemed to be one abode of happiness I grieve to think how quickly the scene changed. Our home was so happy until . . . No, I will not write of that dark time. Suffice it to say it fills my soul with a bitterness that will remain forever. I cannot *forget* & I cannot *forgive*." Even after thirteen years, Catharine mourned for the strength of her father and the peaceful, secure home life she remembered.[54]

The journal that William Johnson kept was a remarkable document that is an unrivaled diary of the life and world of one free man of color. William's journals included very few comments about his family or their social life in Natchez. It was much more a detailed accounting of his business affairs. He began his journal in 1835 when he was approximately twenty-five years old. It ended only with his death in 1851. Catharine's journal, on the other hand, was only kept sporadically over a ten-year period. Her father's journals cover hundreds of pages, Catharine's only forty-five. Her father's is mostly business while her's is filled with personal insights. She wrote in her dairy as a means of coping with her sometimes confusing and overwhelming feelings; her diary was her friend. "Old friend," she wrote on August 2, 1865, "I seldom come to thee except in moments of unhappy thought and feeling when such thoughts as I can not express to a human being like myself." She compared the melancholy sounds of the wind and the rain with her own feelings in her first entry. "Hark, how the rain falls sadly on the housetop and the wind howls. Oh, how mournfully . . . To me it sounds like the Cries of sorrow." Catharine correctly recognized that the sounds reflected her mood. "Yet I love the sound for at present it becomes well my feelings which are like the day, gloomy and sad."[55]

Even though Catharine rarely wrote of anything other than her most private thoughts, she could not ignore the war that raged around her. Writing on New Year's Day 1865, Catharine wrote that things in Natchez changed "evry year, aye evry day and we are of the world and must expect to bear its changes however sad." Later in the same entry she wondered about the safety of her friends. "Ah well, I wonder where Mr Gardner and Mr Reed and the rest of them are to night though if reports be true they are at Savanah and the Confederacy has received another blow. Oh when will this cruel and bloody war end and how. We can only pray Gods will be done at termination." Catharine's confusion about the causes of the war is abundantly clear. "As why it was sent upon the land, none can tell. It is a subject that bafles me completely. Oh, the miserable thought that is conjured up by the mere mention of war." [56]

Neither is her confusion difficult to understand. Catharine would have intimately understood much about the degradation of slavery. Her mother, father, aunt, and grandmothers were freed slaves, so even though she had not experienced firsthand the extreme impediments of slavery, she would have learned about the condition of slavery from her elders. Surely her grandmothers, who had spend most of their lives as slaves, would have related their experiences to their grandchildren. It is impossible not to believe that her parents told her and her siblings how difficult it had been for them to gain their freedom and how threatening their status as slaves had been. While the elders' owners, who might have been their fathers, wished to free their slaves, the state of Mississippi had stringent laws to prevent such manumissions. And what if their owners had died or turned on them for some unknown reason. As long as they remained in slavery, they had no control over their day-to-day lives nor over their destinies. Furthermore, it appears that in 1840 Harriett Battles purchased another slave, Julia, described as a mulatto about twenty-four years of age, along with Julia's two children, Laura, about eleven, and Margaret, an infant, both mulattoes — in order to free them. No free people in Natchez could have understood the consequences of slavery and freedom more than the Johnsons. Indeed, as free people of color, tied to slavery through the color of their skin, neither the Johnsons of Natchez nor the Millers of New Orleans were ever able to fully escape the full implications of slavery. [57]

Yet, both the Johnson and Miller branches of the family knew slavery from another perspective, for they, too, like so many other free people of color in the region, were slaveholders. William Johnson's journal and other papers reveal that most of the members of the family became slaveholders. Certainly William and Ann Johnson freely bought and sold slaves, as well as James and Adelia Miller and Harriett Battles. William Johnson and James Miller bought some slaves and apprenticed others, teaching them the barbering trade. One of William Johnson's slave apprentices (as previously mentioned) was with him on the evening he was shot near Hard Scrabble. Furthermore, a notation in William's journal demonstrates that one of the house slaves of the family refused to obey him and that he had threatened to take the whip to her. Ann also continued to own slaves after William's death. It appears that she had always depended entirely on slaves to market the produce she cultivated in the family's garden and the goods she produced within the household. The family understood the personal degradation of slavery at the same time that they understood it as the basis of the region's economic system.

Indeed, it is clear from Ann's account books and Catharine's diary that the loss of the family's slaves as a result of the war dealt the family a formidable economic blow. A notation penciled into the margins of one of Ann's notebooks revealed that several slaves had left as early as July 1863. One had taken "himself off on a yankee boat. John left on the 27th of the same month. On Monday Cindy left on the same month. On Thursday old Sylvia left on the 1st of August on Sat 1863." Catharine noted in her diary on September 16, 1864, that their slave Jim had come with the news that "Clifton had gone off with some recruiting Officer. We was in hopes that he would never leave us, but turned out like everything, to be all hopes. I suppose it is no use grieving after spilt milk." [58] Because Clifton had been with the family for most of his life, Catharine and her family hoped that he would remain loyal and stay with them. The family's acceptance of slaveholding as a system of labor was obviously not shared by Clifton. He had stayed with the family even as several of their other slaves deserted them in 1863. But by 1864, Clifton saw his chance to escape the bonds of slavery by enrolling in the Union Army.

The Union Army offered freedom through enlistment to any slave who deserted Rebel masters. Another of Ann's slaves had chosen the same route a year earlier when he had left Natchez on a Yankee gunboat. Besides their own freedom, slaves could fight for the freedom of others, and they derived other immediate benefits from army service. The income they would receive must have added to their desire to escape their degraded positions, no matter how close they were to their former owners. Slaves who deserted to join the Union received seven dollars per month with an additional three dollars for clothing. While this was less than what white enlistees received, it was a beginning. Besides their salaries, soldiers were supposed to receive a bounty when they joined. However, many black enlistees were defrauded out of all or part of this bounty. By 1864 when Clifton joined the Union Army to fight for the end of slavery, he joined nearly 150,000 ex-slaves.

After Clifton left, the family faced losing other slaves. In September 1865 Catharine whote that "[s]ome of Sicily's relations has sent for her. I hope that she will not leave us for though she is not very handy she seems willing and that goes a long ways to make one satisfied with a servant. And another thing, Sicily has grown very trifling and at time very insolent if it was not that Ma has had her so long she would soon set her a drift. I think it would come hard with us to part with Maria though." [59]

The war brought economic worries to the family as well. They not only lost the income of their slaves, they had to depend on free laborers in order to survive. On January 1, 1865, Catharine noted that their Christmas table lacked "not many of its accoustomed luxeries; yet some how they were partaken of with the same zest as in former years." Then, near the end of the war on Saturday, March 11, 1865, while the family was struggling to put food on the table, Catharine wrote in her journal "I arose early, it being my week to bake, and set about it with a good will." After baking a number of pies, Catharine sent one of the family servants, Forest, to the docks to sell them. "That day," Catharine wrote, "a number of trips had come down the River and landed here for awhile." The travelers, however, according to Catharine, "proved to be of a very reckless character." [60] Forest returned in a very short time, to Catharine's horror, with none of the pies and with none of the income from them. Did the travelers rob Forest of his pies, or did he sell them and pocket the income? It seems clear from the tone of Catharine's writings that she did not know what happened either to the fruit of her labor or to its possible income. It is also clear, though, that the family no longer controlled its laborers through the methods of intimidation, and threats of violence they had employed before.

Shortly after the end of the war as the family fought to regain their economic footing, Ann Battles Johnson, Anna's and Catharine's mother, died. The pages of Catharine's journal remain silent during those weeks in 1866 that surround her mother's death; consequently, we do not get an account of Ann's death. And neither does Catharine comment on her sister Anna's taking charge of the family household. Anna, it appears, was the logical choice to take charge. Neither William nor Richard, her older brothers, were physically or emotionally able to accept the challenges that such a large family posed. William was diagnosed as insane and institutionalized in New Orleans shortly after his mother's death, and Richard had been weakened by a heart condition. Byron, Catharine, Alice, Josephine, and Clarence were all still too young.

Anna had little difficulty accepting responsibility, and her family probably never doubted her abilities. The earliest description of Anna verified her strength and her competence. In March 1841, William wrote in his journal that "to Day about ———— OClock my Little Daughter was Born And the Larges & Finest Child I Ever saw of its Age — mrs Dickson was with

Her, Ann was well at Dinner time." Her father's first observation was an astute one, for Anna seemed to excel at whatever task was before her. Anna's family and friends clearly recognized her as the most competent of the siblings.[61]

Anna received letters from her cousins in New Orleans, but only two of them can be found in the collection. Both were from Anna's cousin Octavia. It is not difficult to believe that the women wrote more frequently than that and that the letters have been lost. But neither is it difficult to believe that the women lost touch with one another. One letter that Octavia wrote to Anna in 1868 suggests that the women were indeed losing touch. In one passage of the letter Octavia asks Anna to tell Kate (Catharine) "that her love — is allways Accepted — if she remembers me — give her My love — ." [62]

Family circumstances changed dramatically after Anna took charge of the family. Yet neither Ann's death nor Anna's leadership had as much effect on the circumstances of the family as did the conditions left by the war. Just after the war ended, the family depended on peddling produce and other goods, on tutoring, and on farming. By the 1870s the women had begun to turn to sharecropping and teaching to support the family. In 1874 Anna, Catharine, Alice, and Josephine purchased Peachland Plantation and entered into a sharecropping lease with five freed slaves. In the same decade the women had also begun to supplement their income by putting their educations to work. Both Anna and Catharine possessed educations equal to that of most elite white women. Records indicate that Anna, along with her brother William, had been schooled in New Orleans. Catharine, as well as Richard and Byron, were apparently tutored in Natchez. There is no evidence that there were any institutions of education for the children of free people of color in Natchez before the war; few schools were available for free people of color anywhere in the South. Most of those that did exist were in New Orleans, and many of those were Catholic. Sometimes the children of free people of color were taught by family members or by other free people of color, but most were tutored by whites. A family friend, James McCary taught Catharine, Byron, and Richard in Natchez. The children learned musical skills from other tutors in the community. Even though Anna was schooled in New Orleans, and Catharine was educated in Natchez, both women had been taught the basics in mathematics and geography, English literature, and the French language.[63]

Catharine and Anna knew the importance of education. Catharine mentioned the strain William's incapacitation put on the family and the education of her younger siblings. She wrote in her journal that "if it was not for William and his family, which he has brought here for us to provide for, our circumstances would be much better and the children might receive a chance of an education, which is their right." Instead of that, she continued, "the burden of the other family (for William does not provide for them) — and such a family — is a heavy weight on her [Anna's] slender income. And prevents her giving them anything like an education. My heart swells with indignation and a bitter, bitter feeling of resentment towards him when I look at them and think for his sake they are growing up in ignorance."[64]

It was to their educations and to the improvement of others that Catharine and Anna Johnson eventually turned for the financial support of themselves and their family. After schools were opened for the freed slaves during reconstruction in Mississippi, the women obtained teaching jobs. Both women began teaching in Natchez in 1870. That was when, on January 10, 1870, the city council of Natchez appointed seven white men as the board of directors of the "committee on colored schools." The council also approved expenditures for the school not to exceed three hundred dollars a month. Catharine taught freed slaves in the Union School until she moved to Ravenwood, where she taught until her retirement. Anna taught for the Union School from 1870 until her retirement in 1906 or 1907. Both women were second-grade teachers. Both brought their considerable talent and skills into the classroom, providing pupils and colleagues with a first-class example of spirit and dedication to future generations. The letters between them are valuable for information they give of the schools for people of color in late nineteenth-century Mississippi.[65]

The letters and diary in this collection are extraordinary for what they demonstrate about a particular group of heretofore obscure women — the free women of color of the South. That is not to suggest that the experiences and identities of these women exactly represent those of other free women of color, for they do not. Even the women represented in the pages of this collection did not experience the world around them in the same way. Their experiences as women who were attached to slavery through race, and yet were free, varied, one from the other. Harriett Battles and Amy Johnson spent much of their lives as slaves. They knew the pain of bringing children into slavery. Their children, Ann Battles Johnson and Adelia (Miller) and William Johnson, were born into slavery but were freed as children. That had to have made their knowledge of the world of slavery around them fundamentally different from that of their mothers. And their children, the children of Ann and Adelia, were born into freedom and thus even further removed from slavery. It was these children who escaped the worst that the slave system had to offer. Yet, even though none of these women experienced slavery and freedom in the same way, their letters and diary tell us much about the free women of color in the South who did not leave clear records of their lives. There are fundamental issues of race, gender, and condition that are played out in the lives of these women that would have been central to any free women of color. It is to these issues that this collection speaks.

NOTES

1. There is no evidence that Harriett Battles could write. In fact, to the contrary, she sent messages and conducted her business through her son-in-law William Johnson and her daughter Ann.

2. Adélia and William Johnson were the only children of Amy Johnson of Natchez. Ann was the only daughter of Harriett Battles.

3. Lavinia Miller to Ann Johnson, December 2, 1848; the William Johnson journal, July 24, 1837. Both from the William T. Johnson Family Collection, Hill Memorial Library, Louisiana State University. Hereafter cited as the W. T. Johnson Collection.

4. D. Clayton James, *Antebellum Natchez* (Louisiana State University Press, Baton Rouge, 1968), 183–216.

5. Catherine Clinton, *The Plantation Mistress* (New York: Pantheon Books, 1982); Ann Firor Scott, *The Southern Lady: From Pedestal to Politics* (Chicago: The University of Chicago Press, 1970); Suzanne Lebsock, *The Free Women of Petersburg: Status and Culture in a Southern Town, 1784–1860* (New York: Norton, 1984).

6. An excellent book that explores these issues is Deborah Gray White, *Ar'n't I a Woman: Female Slaves in the Antebellum South* (New York: W. W. Norton, 1985).

7. Virginia Meacham Gould, "In Full Enjoyment of their Freedom: The Free Women of Color of the Gulf Ports of New Orleans, Mobile, and Pensacola, 1769–1860, Ph.D. diss., Emory University, 1991.

8. Adams County Marriage Records, vol. 542; diary entry April 21, 1836. The marriage license is included in the W. T. Johnson Papers. The courtship's beginnings also can be found in the papers in a letter from Washington Sterns to William Johnson, March 6, 1829.

9. The journal of William T. Johnson, W. T. Johnson Collection.

10. Evidence for the family's accumulation of slaves can be found in William Johnson's journal, W. T. Johnson Collection. According to the Natchez tax records of 1844, the Johnsons owned eight slaves. In 1850 the city tax records indicate that they had five slaves; in 1857, after William Johnson's death, Ann Johnson paid taxes on six slaves. Evidently, Ann's slaveholdings grew because in 1860 she paid the taxes on seven slaves,

and in 1861 she paid taxes on eight slaves. The net worth of her slaves in 1861 was six thousand dollars.

11. Ann Johnson's account books, entries recorded March–October 1855, W. T. Johnson Collection.

12. Notebook, vol. 38, July 1844–1857, William T. Johnson Family Papers, Hill Memorial Library, Louisiana State University (LSU).

13. William Johnson's journal, July 29, 1836, and December 2, 1836, W. T. Johnson Collection.

14. William Johnson's journal and the day books of Ann Johnson, W. T. Johnson Collection.

15. The Johnson family papers contain various notebooks with examples of the repetitive school work of the children. A notation in vol. 37, March 1857–1859, reveals that Anna began music lessons on March 17, 1857. Also, see Lawrence W. Minor to Mrs. William Johnson, March 12, 1853; William Johnson Jr. to Mrs. William Johnson, May 14, 1853; receipt for tuition of two children, April 3, 1853, signed by N. Morton, the William Johnson Family Papers, Hill Memorial Library, LSU.

16. Letter from Adelia Johnson to William T. Johnson, February 16, 1844; a letter from Octavia Miller to Ann Battles Johnson, December 1847, W. T. Johnson Collection.

17. Harriett Battles was the daughter of the free woman of color Jane (Jenny) Bush, who had been freed in Concordia Parish, Louisiana, in 1819. Jane lived in Natchez until 1840. See certificates of freedom signed by J. Robataille, June 11, 1840, and by Horace Gridley, June 26, 1840. W. T. Johnson Collection. The petitions for the manumission of Harriett and Ann Battles are found in folder 15, W. T. Johnson Collection.

18. Charles S. Sydnor, "The Free Negro in Mississippi Before the Civil War," *American Historical Review*, 32 (July 1927): 771–79.

19. Gould, "In Full Enjoyment of Their Freedom"; Kimberly Hanger, "Personas de Varias Colores," Ph.D. diss., University of Florida, 1991; Gwendolyn Midlo Hall, *Africans in Colonial New Orleans: The Development of Afro-Creole Culture in the Eighteenth Century* (Baton Rouge: Louisiana State University Press, 1992).

20. Emancipation records, May 14, 1814, Vidalia, Louisiana.

21. Notarial records, June 25, 1882, Vidalia, Louisiana.

22. Property records, County Courthouse, Cincinnati, Ohio, April 27, 1826.

23. Records of the state legislature, February 10, 1820, Jackson, Mississippi. William Johnson's tombstone states that he was born in 1809.

24. Census for the Territory of Mississippi, Adams County, 1800; Census for the Territory of Mississippi, Adams County, 1810; 1820 U.S. Census, State of Mississippi, City of Natchez; 1830 U.S. Census, State of Mississippi, City of Natchez; 1840 U.S. Census, State of Mississippi, City of Natchez; 1850 U.S. Census, State of Mississippi, City of Natchez; 1860 U.S. Census, State of Mississippi, City of Natchez.

25. 1840 U.S. Census, State of Mississippi, Adams County, City of Natchez; 1850 U.S. Census, State of Mississippi, Adams County, City of Natchez.

26. Ira Berlin, *Slaves without Masters: The Free Negro in the Antebellum South* (New York: Oxford University Press, 1981), 86–89. Annals of Congress, 1st Cong., 2d sess., 1453–64.

27. Sydnor, "The Free Negro in Mississippi," 771–79.

28. *Natchez*, March 5, 1831, William T. Johnson's journal. W. T. Johnson Collection.

29. *Courier*, August 7, 1841, Natchez Public Library.

30. *Natchez Free Trader*, August 17, 1841, Natchez Public Library.

31. William Johnson's journal, August 17 and 18, 1841, W. T. Johnson Collection.

32. William Johnson's journal, September 5, 1841, W. T. Johnson Collection.

33. William Johnson's journal, July 9 and 10, 1842, W. T. Johnson Collection.

34. William Johnson's journal, July 9, 1842, W. T. Johnson Collection.

35. William Johnson's journal, July 9, 1842, W. T. Johnson Collection.

36. J. S. Buckingham, *The Slave States of America* (London: Fisher, Son & Co., 1842), 479–88.

37. Ann and William Johnson had their oldest son, William Robert Johnson, baptized at the St. Louis Cathedral March 31, 1842. His baptism is recorded in the Register of Baptisms, Slaves and Free People of Color, January 1841–December 1842, vol. 30. William Johnson's journal, July 9 and 10, 1842, W. T. Johnson Collection.

38. The baptism records of Benedict Byron Johnson born June 22, 1839; Clement Richard Johnson born October 11, 1837; and Ann Johnson born March 25, 1841, can be found in the W. T. Johnson Collection and in the Baptismal Register of Slaves and Free People of Color, 1842–56, vol. 32, St. Louis Cathedral. A trip was made to New Orleans in 1848 to baptize the child Louis Johnson. Louis was born November 28, 1846, but he must have died shortly after his baptism as he is not mentioned in other family records. His baptism was recorded as "Louis Jonsen, son of Guilliame Johnsen and Ann Battles," Register of Baptisms, Slaves and Free People of Color, vol. 33. A final trip was made to New Orleans to baptize Marie Alice Johnson, born April 1842; Catharine Johnson, born December 22, 1843; Eugenia Johnson, born January 2, 1845; Josephine Johnson born July 29, 1849; and Gabriel Clarence Johnson, born May 16, 1851. Their baptisms were recorded June 5, 1856, in the Baptismal Register of Whites, 1848–57, vol. 20.

39. Roger Baudier, *The Catholic Church in Louisiana* (New Orleans, 1939; rpt., Louisiana Library Assoc., 1972), 179–246. Records of the St. Louis Cathedral, New Orleans.

40. Baptismal Records of the St. Louis Cathedral, June 13, 1856.

41. Letter, October 2, 1847, W. T. Johnson Collection.

42. Letter, May 20, 1855, W. T. Johnson Collection.

43. Letter, March 11, 1855, W. T. Johnson Collection.

44. William Johnson's journal, January 1848, W. T. Johnson Collection.

45. Several years after Adelia's death, her son James died. The death records for the family are located in Records of Deaths, City of New Orleans, New Orleans Public Library. The cemetery records can be found at the Louisiana Historical Center, New Orleans. Adelia Miller's death is recorded in The Health Dept. Records of New Orleans, January 9, 1848.

46. Natchez *Courier*, June 17, 1851.

47. For a detailed look at William Johnson's death and the trials that followed it, see William Ransom-Hogan and Edwin Adams Davis, *The Barber of Natchez* (Baton Rouge: Louisiana State University Press, 1954), 262–72.

48. Adams County Tax Records for 1860, Adams County Courthouse.

49. Leonard Curry, *The Free Black in Urban America, 1800–1850* (Chicago: University of Chicago Press, 1981), 1–14.

50. Account book, 1854–1866, W. T. Johnson Collection; also see loose receipts.

51. Account books and loose receipts, W. T. Johnson Collection. By 1857 Ann Johnson was paying taxes on four houses. See tax records, City of Natchez.

52. Account books, loose receipts, and loose papers, W. T. Johnson Collection.

53. Account books and loose receipts, W. T. Johnson Collection.

54. Catharine Geraldine Johnson's diary, May 10, 1864, W. T. Johnson Collection.

55. Catharine Geraldine Johnson's diary, W. T. Johnson Collection.

56. Catharine Geraldine Johnson's diary, W. T. Johnson Collection.

57. Deed of purchase for Julia Ann, Laura, and Margaret, dated January 28, 1840. The slaves were purchased from Miles Kelly. W. T. Johnson Collection.

58. Catharine Geraldine Johnson's diary, W. T. Johnson Collection.

59. Catharine Geraldine Johnson's diary, September 24, 1865, W. T. Johnson Collection.

60. Catharine Geraldine Johnson's diary, W. T. Johnson Collection.

61. Anna L. Johnson was born March 25, 1841. She was baptized Ann Johnson and was known as Anna L. Johnson in her later years; quote from William Johnson's journal, March 25, 1841, W. T. Johnson Collection. The date of Anna Johnson's birth is also recorded on her baptismal certificate. Anna died November 25, 1922. Adams County Probate Records, no. 5,618, file 313. Adams County Will Books, vol. 7, 306–7.

62. Letters, 1868, W. T. Johnson Collection.

63. A letter dated March 12, 1853, from a school in New Orleans states that William Johnson Jr. studied arithmetic, geography, and grammar with Laurence W. Viven. A receipt for tuition for schooling for two children paid to N. Norton, July 17, 1854, by Mrs. Johnson is included in the loose records of the W. T. Johnson Collection. An entry in a notebook dated August 22, 1855, states that Ann Johnson had remitted $3.50 to Mr. McCary for Byron and William's schooling. An entry in the daybook dated January 1851–1867 states that Byron commenced going to school at Mr. McCary's on July 28, 1856. A ledger dated March 1857–May 1859 states that Kate had left home that morning for her school in Louisiana. The same sum, $3.50, was paid in September. A notation dated October 29, 1855, says that "I paid Bener for music lessons for the two girls." The same notations can be found for several months. Ledger, vol. 41, W. T. Johnson Collection. Ann wrote in a notebook on January 10, 1856, that Richard had gone to work in order to learn the blacksmith trade. Ann and William's youngest son also learned the blacksmith trade. Free men of color in the Gulf Coast cities often dominated the barbering and blacksmithing trades. The purchase agreement for Peachland and the sharecropping agreement are found in loose papers, W. T. Johnson Collection.

64. Catharine at this time did not know the seriousness of William's mental illness. It was only later that the family had to have him committed and placed under the guardianship of an old family friend. March 11, 1865, Catharine Geraldine Johnson's diary, W. T. Johnson Collection.

65. Minutes of the City Council of Natchez, January 1870. Teacher Register and Teacher Pay Certificates, 1874–1915. The certificates of Anna and Catharine are located in the W. T. Johnson Collection. Josephine Johnson, the sister of Anna and Catharine, later joined her sisters and taught at the Union School.

HARRIETT BATTLES was born in approximately 1792. She was the slave of Gabriel Tichenor until 1822 when she was freed. She was the mother of Ann Battles Johnson; Tichenor was most likely Ann's father. Harriett died in 1873.

AMY JOHNSON was the slave of Capt. William Johnson until he freed her in 1814. Johnson freed Amy's children, Adelia and William, a few years later. Captain Johnson was probably the father of Amy's children as he remained close to the family throughout his lifetime.

ANN BATTLES JOHNSON was born in 1815. She was the daughter of Harriett Battles. Ann married William T. Johnson on April 21, 1835. She died in 1866.

ADELIA JOHNSON MILLER was born in 1806; she was the daughter of Amy Johnson and the sister of William T. Johnson. She married James Miller and moved with him to New Orleans in 1829. She died January 8, 1848.

WILLIAM T. JOHNSON was Amy's son. Adelia was his only sibling. William Johnson's tombstone reads that he was born in 1809, and he died in 1851.

JAMES MILLER was born free in Philadelphia in 1816. He moved to Mississippi in 1816 and married Adelia Johnson. James was a barber by trade and took Adelia's young brother, William, as his apprentice. James and Adelia moved to New Orleans in 1829, where James died on July 8, 1865.

The Children of Ann Battles Johnson and William T. Johnson
> WILLIAM JR., born January 24, 1836
> RICHARD, born October 11, 1837
> BYRON, born June 22, 1839
> ANNA, born March 25, 1841
> ALICE, born April 16, 1842

CATHARINE, born December 22, 1843

PHILLIP, born in 1844; he died shortly after birth

EUGENIA, born January 2, 1845

LOUIS, born November 28, 1846

JOSEPHINE, born August 5, 1849

CLARENCE, born May 16, 1851

The Children of Adelia Johnson Miller and James Miller

CATHARINE, born in 1828

WILLIAM, born in 1830

JAMES, born in 1832

LAVINIA, born in 1834

EMMA, born in 1836

OCTAVIA, born in 1838

VERENE, born in 1840

Unnamed child, born in 1842 but died soon after birth

ALBERT, born in 1845

The Prewar Family Letters
of the Johnson-Miller Women
of Natchez *and* New Orleans

New Orleans January 2nd 1844

Dear Brother

Your letter of the 27th came safe to hand today.[1] But not By Mr Potter as it states. Wellington[2] gave it to me and he says Charles gave it to him. It gave me great Pleasure to heare from you all wonce More and heare that you are all well as this Leaves us all. You Complain About my not writing. I find it useless to write to you all. For William, you have the Most Neglegent set of Boys About you that I ever saw. We could not get along with them one Month. Now those Mats that you Speak of. I gave [them] to William Nix and A Barrel of oysters for you and Mother[3] and Beg him to give the Mats to [you] and the oysters to Mother to Be devided and he did not do it. This Letter that I received to day Looks as if it has Been Lying in A Brushheap. I am Surprised at you for not keeping Better regulations About you. And the sage I got after Lying in your shop I dont know how Long. I wrote A Letter to Mother and ask her to send me Some Spar ribs. But she did not think it worth her while to do so. No its not my fault in the Least. I wish you ware half as readay as I am. It would do. My Cow is quite well and gives me three Bits worth of Milk every day. I wish it was ice cream time now. Those Turkeys you sent me and Mr Johnson.[4] We got them safe and I think I Mention them in my Last Letter that I wrote you. Tell Bill Nix[5] that tale he told up thare About being in the Calaboose is a whoper. And to mend the Matter, he had to Link young Yebreska in it. He would not thank him for it if he knew it. Bob Smith[6] told me About it to day. He call to see me. I told him that it was no such thing. It was some of William own make.

No More at Present. Give my Love to all.

I received some meal By Wellington and he says he dont know who sent it. How ever I return my thanks for it.

I remain your
Affc Sister
AD Miller

1. This letter is the earliest in the collection; although an earlier letter from Adelia was cited in William Ransom Hogan and Edwin Adams Davis, *The Ante-Bellum Diary of a Free Negro* (Baton Rouge: Louisiana State University Press, 1951).

2. Wellington West was the slave of James Miller and Adelia Johnson Miller of New Orleans. He usually worked in New Orleans for the Millers, but occasionally he worked in Natchez for the Johnsons. On February 17, 1847, William noted in his journal that he

had "sent Mrs. Miller To Day $20.00 being the Sum due To Her for Middleton's wages up to the 8th or 10th of March, next month — This settlement is for five months up to the 9th of next month Leaving Out two weeks that He Lost, the amount of which is $72. I Took out $52 for Doctors Bills that I paid out of the money — $32 to Dr. Hogg & 20 Dollars to Dr Hubbard — deductin Both of there Bills Leaves a Ballance in her favor of twenty Dollars, which I sent to Her as I Stated above by Mr Tosspitt." In December 1866, Wellington West testified at a hearing to determine the distribution of the estate of James Miller that he had known James Miller and that they had been residents of New Orleans for thirty-five to forty years. James Miller, he stated, "had raised me and learned me my trade."

3. "Mother" was Amy Johnson, the mother of William Johnson and Adelia Johnson Miller.

4. Mr. (William) Johnson was the previous owner of Amy Johnson and her two children, William and Adelia. It has been speculated that he was their white father, and because he remained close to both William and Adelia throughout his lifetime, it is probable that he was.

5. William (Bill) Nix was a free man of color living in Natchez. He was much younger than William Johnson and, in fact, was apprenticed to Johnson for some time. Despite his close attachment to Nix, Johnson regularly complained about Nix's behavior in his journal. In one instance, Johnson complained that Nix (who was described by Johnson as light complected) had been wrongfully yielding to the charms of black slave women. Johnson's business relationship with Nix appears to have extended for at least five years, from 1839 to 1844.

6. Robert Smith was a free man of color. He was first a resident of New Orleans but had moved to Natchez after being charged with buying goods from a slave. When Smith stood trial in Natchez in 1837 in order to determine whether he could remain in the state, Johnson refused to defend Smith, saying that he was wrong to press his point to stay in Natchez and make others (free people of color) suffer for it.

New Orleans Feb the 16th, 1844

Dear Brother

I take my pen in hand to address you a few lines in answer to your last letter and to let you know that we are all well at present, hoping that you are the same. You must excuse me for not writing to you sooner. I would of answered your letter by the same boat, but the pig that mother sent me was so fine that Miller invited two or three of his friends to dine with him and so I had to prepare dinner for them. It was really a fine pig and you will please tell mother that I thank her a thousand times for it. Tell her that her health was drank and the health of all her boys also. I have nothing knew to relate you that I have'nt. In contemplation to send my two boys[1] away with young Yebreska to school in Kingston and Mr Miller talks of going with them and wants you to accompany him, but wether he does or not I think I shall take and send them there. They will get a trade. Also, if you cant go, you had better send Bucks. Those boys are getting very troublesome. Little Mrs. Johnson is here from across the Lake.[2] She has been here for a week and her husband has just returned from England. You ought to see them. They have made up and it is laughable to see them going all about lock arm and he looking for all the world like old jack tar. I have tryed to shame them out of it but it is no use.

Ask Bill Nix what he done with the money I gave him to get the oysters — a dollar and a half.

I suppose that you heard that old french William is to be married in May to one of Norman Davises daughter that is now staying with old Johnson[3] and you would be diverted to heare the Courtship for William cant keep his own secrets.

No more at present. Give my love to all the family, and expect the same yourself.

AD Miller

Those Log Cabin seal that you seal your letters with is to easy open. A word to the wise is a nuft.[4]

1. Adelia Miller's two young sons were James and William. James was the oldest child of James and Adelia Miller. He was sixteen in 1844 when his mother wrote this letter; he died in New Orleans on February 24, 1848. William was born in 1830 in Natchez and was fourteen years old in 1844 when his mother was contemplating sending the boys away to school. William died on May 6, 1855 in New Orleans.

2. Lake Pontchartrain.

3. French William was a free man of color, an apprentice of William Johnson. Old Johnson was probably the white William Johnson, originally the owner of Amy, Adelia, and William Johnson.

4. Better than any other statement in these letters, Adelia's warning to her brother that the seals on his letters were easy to open sufficiently demonstrates the concern for privacy and safety that the free-colored community of the Gulf South was experiencing by the 1840s.

New Orleans, Nov the 6 1844

Dear Brother

I write you these few lines to inform you that we are all well at present, hoping that you are the same. I will not tresspass on your time by writing a long letter. This is merly to ask if you saw that meal that you sent down to me. I cant think that you did and this is the reason that I write to you is I dont think you ever saw worst meal in all your life. We cannot do ennything with it at all. I bought a bushel from the carts this morning as they went along. I did not send you the mony this trip as I did not know what it was. But you will let me know by Wellington and I will send it up.

Give My love to Mother and all the family and expect the same yourself.

I remain your Sincerely Sister
AD Miller

New Orleans Oct 2nd 1847

Mrs. Anna[1] Johnson delivered by the politeness of Mr. Lee

I write you these few lines to inform you that we are all well at present esccept Little verania[2] and she is still down with that foot. And I am glad to hear that you are injoying your healths. Those things you sent Me came safe to hand and the stockings I found since I wrote you so I believe thaier is nothing els that I can think of. And that quilt, I am sorry that it is sold. The others you know she ask more for so I think I will have some of those comforts made and that will answer my purpose as well. If she will let me have the other one for the same prise you can take it. If not let it alone. Give my love to William and tell him that all thing will be alright and Arrange to his satisfaction and he must get those doc Bills and send them down. The reason that Mr. Miller did not right the last trip he says he thought I wrote every thing that he wished to say and I thought he wrote so we were Both out of it.

Ask Mother to try and get me some eggs if she can and send them down by this boat. They are four [bits] a doz here and not good at that.

Gave my love to all and the same youre self

AD Miller[3]

1. This letter was sent to Ann Johnson. It appears that her nickname, like that of her daughter after her, was Anna.

2. Verania (also known as "Verene" and "Verena") Miller was the daughter of Adelia and James Miller. She was approximately twelve years old in 1844.

3. This is the last letter in the collection that was written by Adelia. She died on Sunday, January 9, 1848, of tuberculosis. The record of Adelia's death can be found in the New Orleans Health Dept. Records, vol. 10, p. 511, New Orleans Public Library. Adelia was described in the record of her death as forty-two years old. She was buried in Girod Street Cemetery in New Orleans. Her burial record can be found in the sacramental records of Christ Cathedral Episcopal Church in New Orleans.

New Orleans, December the 2nd
1848

Dear Aunt

I write to you these few lines to inform you that I received you wellcom letter and was glad to hear that your self and children are enjoying good health as these few lines now leave my self and sisters and brothers. I also received the eggs and cloth and bonnet that you sent me and I am a thousand times oblige to you for them untill you are better paid. If you want anything dont lack sending for it. Any thing I can get for you I will do it with pleasure. Madame Amie[1] was here last week and she was on her way looking for another house. The one she had was too small. She wants to rent furnished rooms and now she has found a larger one. Manda[2] is married to a white man last saturday night. Madame Amie was not at the wedding nor her sister Kittey. None but the family — and not all of them. Her mother says that the man has been courtin her eight years and she told me that he was going to bay of St. Louis to marry becaus they could not get lawful married here. That was to fool me. But madame Amie told me that they did not go. That they had the French Priest to make the serremony at the house without licens. Now what you call that.[3]

Welingtons boat is sunk but I got all my things you sent to me.

Give my love to grand-ma[4] and tell her that I will write to her next trip. Give my love to Uncle William and to William and to all the children and your mother.

Tell William he must write to me. No more at present. I remain your affectionate niece.

Lavinia Miller

Will sends his love to you.

1. Madame Anriese Amie was a free woman of color and a close and personal friend of Adelia Miller and Ann Johnson. She was married to James McCary, the son of Robert McCary, on October 19, 1852.

2. "Manda" is Amanda Brustee, who was a free woman of color and the daughter of Charlotte and Gabriel Brustee.

3. It was not unusual for free women of color and white men from New Orleans to go to Mississippi to marry. Some, however, were married by the city's French priests, as suggested by this letter. This marriage, however, was without benefit of license, which meant it was not legally recognized. The couple's marriage was illegal in Louisiana; thus

it was only recognized in the laws of the church. The record of this union can be found in the marriage records of the St. Louis Cathedral.

4. Amy Johnson, William and Adelia Johnson's mother and Lavinia's grandmother, died in Natchez on January 6, 1849.

 _____

New Orleans November 2, 184—[1]

Dear Aunt

I write you these few lines to inform you that I received your wellcome letter and was happy to hear that your self and family is enjoying good health as these few lines now leave myself and sisters and brothers. And Cathriene is very well and is going to Mary Jordans house to play. Ellen was here yesterday and spent the evening with us. I received the dress and apron and night gown for cathrien and the pepper and I am very much oblige to you. I have sent the little shawl up by jef. I had not time to go and get the calico but I will send it next trip. Kate[2] sends her love to all the children. Give my love to william and all the children. Emma had not time to write you to this trip. Kiss Joe[3] for me and Alice. Give my love to your ma. Jef is waiting for my letter. If you see Julia tell her that I had not time to answer her letter, but will answer it next week. I heard mag was to be married to bill hoggett. Is it true. I must stop. No more at present. I remain you scincer neice Lavinia Miller You ought to of broke old Mrs coalmans neck out of your yard.

LM

1. The date of this letter is incomplete, but it appears to have been written in 1849.
2. Catherine Geraldine Johnson.
3. Josephine Johnson, the youngest daughter of William and Ann Johnson. Josephine was born on August 25, 1849.

 _____

New Orleans December the 6, 18—[1]

Dear Aunt

I take the greates pleasure of Writing you those few lines to inform you that I received your Welcome letter, and What's more We're glad to heare About you and the family. We're injoying good health, as this letter know leaves me in a bad condition, all of the rest of the family is quit well at present. I hope that those few lines may find you in the same state of health. Deare Aunt, I am in so much pain With my face that I could scarcely Write you those few lines. I had a tooth drawn. I did not take care of it and i caught cold in it, my face is swolen all up and it do pane me so bad, but I trust in god that I Will get Well again. I hope, Deare Aunt, I have done the best I could in getting your things that you bid me to get. I got you three Dimes Worth of nutmeg and all so two dimes Worth of cinnamon that is the best that I could Aunt and, I hope that it Will please you fore I did do the best I could. My face pane me so bad that I could not go and price the oysters fore you, but I Will be sure and price them fore you. You say Aunt Ann I had fore my god child. I have not fore I Was this telling mom that I must begin to send man something but the thing has got so deare, I have got hem a Drum for this Week. I will try and get something els fore him. I Would have got something, But Aunt Ann I am in so much With my face. You don't know the pane I am in, but I hope that this Will suit him till I am able to get out and get something els fore him. I am verry glad to heare that you all like the oysters I sent Anna, I expect Anna think that I have keep my Woard this time. I must know send Kate something When I get Well and If nothen hapen and father all so send his respect you and family.

I must know
close my letter by
saying I remain your nice
O. M.[2]

1. The date of this letter is incomplete, but it appears it was written in 1849.
2. Octavia Miller was the fourth child of Adelia and James Miller. She was born in New Orleans where she remained throughout her life. She married Theodule Martin of New Orleans.

 ─────────────────────────────────────

New Orleans July 2nd 1850

Dear Aunt

I take this pleasure of taking my pen in hand to write you few lines to inform you that I well and also my father are enjoying good health. I was very happy indeed to return home and find him well, at present. the Natchez No 2 got in very early. She got in here thursday evening at half pas six O clock, and we have had great deal of rain and warmed weather in the sity, have not much news to relat to you in regard of our sity. all is that the sity very health. no sickness here whatever and all. I wish it will keep so and I hope this letter will find you all enjoying good health. Hir are these lemons I sent you. I like to for got them and if I had to for got them and you would not got them you would go angry with me, but I am very glad that I did not. Did benenj tell you about that fellow Dumain did about him stealing 100 & 50 dollers and now gone to California. he always like he would steal in a minet. Such fellows like them, I dont like to be in there company. I [k]now to many now and I am try my best to keep away from them if can.

I did not get of[f] monday aunt as I thought I would but I have received letter from West saturday had he relate to me that nothing much doing over the lake now and saids that they are very few people now over the lake, but if I dont go over this week I will let you know. I think great many people will being go over about this time or next monnth. Give my best respect to Uncl william and also to reast of the family and also I send my love and wishes to yourself. And allow me to subscribe myself as your sincere

Nephew.
Wm Miller [1]

excuse this bad writeing

1. William Miller was the son of Adelia Johnson Miller and James Miller. He was named after his uncle William Johnson.

New Orleans November the 23, 1850

Dear Aunt

I write you these few lines to inform you that I received your wellcom letter and was very sorry to hear that uncle will was unwell. Tho it was very imprudent on his part to go to that fire and work so. They would not do as much for him. We are all well and enjoying very good health. Thank god and I hope that when you receive that letter uncle william will be well. I have sent you the calico and father got two pair of shose for Kate at sixty five cents a pair. They are good ones. Mrs. Brustee [1] was hear yesterday and her sister and Manda was hear today. She looks so old. I got the three yards for you and the twelve yards and nine in the other. And I have sent you some peaces of my dresses that I bought. The two dark peaces is a dime a yard and the other, the red, is twenty cents a yard and the other is french calico. It is twenty five cents a yard. The boat did not get hear until friday night and I write you this letter in haste giving my love to all. Kate has left some of her things such as a night handkerchief and cap, but I will send these next trip as I am in a hurry now.

no more at present
Lavinia Miller

1. Mrs. Charlotte Brustee was a free woman of color. Originally from Natchez, Madame Brustee was a close friend of Ann Johnson. Upon the death of her husband, Gabriel Brustee, she moved to New Orleans. In the 1840 U.S. Census (State of Louisiana, City of New Orleans) she is described as a widow. In the 1850 census Madame Brustee appears as a forty-five-year-old mulatto with three children: Agla, twenty-five years old, Louisa, twenty-two years old, and Asparie, ten years old; all the children were mulatto. Brustee is spelled in a variety of ways, with the spellings being Brustee and Brustie.

New Orleans Nov 26th, 1850

Dear Mother

I take my pen in hand to write you a few lines to in form you that I am well and all the rest of the family and also hopeing that these few lines may find you and all my sisters and Brothers well at present, but as you complain of my writing you such short letters and of my not telling you any news but it is not because I have forgotten you, but it is because I have none to tell.

I have got my pance but they did not fit. They were too long for me and they were mostly too large in the legs.

Emma sends up some cake for you and some for bena and them kisses for Cathra and that fruit cake also. Emma gives her love anthony, mag, and all of them. Emma says she will write to you next week and also get them Calicos for you. Tell James that them white rabbits was eight dollars a pair and besides emma says she is maried[1] and was married on thursday 24th and jef says please to send him down fifty Dollars by Mr Douce. Tell him not to give it to nobody but him or me. And as I forgot to tell you that the wedding went on first rate and I enjoyed myself very well indeed. Danced just as much as I wished. Give my love to granma and all the rest of the family. Please kiss the little man for me. Tell boys I have not forgot them by no means in the world and also the major.

No more at present, but remain

your affectionate son.
Byron Johnson

1. Emma Miller married Jefferson Hoggatt, a free man of color originally from Natchez. Jefferson, like Emma, was a mulatto. Emma and Jefferson probably met in Natchez since before moving to New Orleans. Jefferson had been apprenticed to William Johnson.

ADDRESSED TO: Miss Anna L Johnson

Prsent

Natchez January 24, 1852

Dear Miss Anna

Henry Green says he will give you $120 for Your mule if you will wate untill the end of the year. He says he take him know. Live or die he will pay you for him. Green leeses ground on the said place for one forth of the cotton & one forth of the corn.

Yours Truly

John Chavours

New Orleans October 26th, 1852

Dear Aunt

I write you these few lines to inform you that we are all well and I hope that these few lines may find you and all the children enjoying the same state of health. I suppose you heard that father arrived home safe and he looks remarkable well. He brought all the likenesses of his sister and her four Daughters.[1] I have a piece of news to tell you that will surpris you that you must not mention it. Well, Annie Amie[2] is married. She got married last wensday and she is four months gone in the family way. The same day her ma found it out she had her married right aft and netter sent for her grandma that was downtown or sent word to her uncle. No one knew of it but her sister-in-law and the young man's grandma and I know that fanny has not heard it. Dont tell her nothing about it. Mrs. Brustee came strait and told me when she heard it. The young man is her cousin too. He is madam Mellions son. They had not one chair bought and he is a high living fellow, aunt. He has a trade, but wont work. Now she will have them both to support. Por Mrs Amie. Mr. Bruistee was so mad that he cried. Aunt, father says please send him a jar of them pickles that you sent by Will. I write you this letter in a hurry.

Give my love to all.

your sincer niece

Lavinia McCary[3]

1. James Miller had returned to Philadelphia, where he was originally from, in order to visit his family.

2. Annie Amie was Madame Amie Brustee's daughter.

3. A note on the back of this letter states that the letter was from Lavina McCary, and it said, "Married October 19th 1852 Annie Amie."

New Orleans March 12th, 1853

Mrs. Johnson:

My dear Madam

William leaves to day to see you and his dear friends at home. I regret the necessity that takes him home at this time. But as its important, I cannot complain. He has been with me a month, and believe me Madam I do not flatter you nor him when I say that I never had anybody make better progress in the same length of time. He commenced Grammer and Geography both of which were new to him. With a little more pains in remembering what he learns, he will soon master them. He is also studying arithmetic which is somewhat difficult for him now. He will, I think, soon get over that. I shall commence soon with him the keeping of accounts. I would add that William is very tractable and willing to be an obedient and good boy. My wife joins me in regard for you and Yours.

Lawrence W. Minen[1]

1. This letter is a report from Lawrence Minen, William's teacher in New Orleans.

New Orleans May 14th, 1853

Dear Mother

I write you these lines to inform you that I am in tolerable good health at present excepting a bad cold and I hope these few lines may find you and all the family in good health. I received your letter and was very glad to hear that you was well. I acknowledge that really feel ashamed of my self to have you think that I have been extravagant my money. I will Confess that I have been simple enough to spend my money very foolishly since I have been down here, but I hope it won't be the case again. I am certain it won't be the case any more because I find it won't pay, for money is two hard to get hold of. I received the shirts that you sent me and is very much obliged to you for them. They was two top shirts and three undershirts. I liked them pretty well. I suppose you will send the other four down next trip. You wrote me word that the excitement was rising again about that trial, as the time was drawing near. I hope the excitement ain't died away on our side and I trust to god he wont get clear. I expect I will have to come up shortly. I was very much pleased to hear how friendly Winston and Byron and Richard is. Tell Jim I received the Tricopherous he sent me and it was very nice indeed. Tell him I would sen something, but he must recollect that I am three hundred miles from home and is pretty near broke. The weather is fine and pleasant, but the times is getting very dull and scarcely any news stiring. You never write me word whether you sold Fanny[1] or not. Give my love to granma and to all the family and to Edward[2] and all my friends.

Nothing more at present
your affecttionate
Wm Johnson

1. A slave belonging to the Johnsons.
2. Edward Hoggatt, a free mulatto apprenticed to William Johnson. He was riding with Johnson when they were ambushed by Baylor Winn. Both Hoggatt and Johnson were shot. Johnson died the next morning; Hoggatt survived the attack.

New Orleans June 4th, 1853

Dear Madam,

I take this opertunity of writing you these few lines to inform you that I am well, hoping that these few lines may find you and your Children in the same state of Health. The Lorde has Blest Me with good Health, tho Madam you Must no that I Must Have my Hands full as a Man to take the Charge of a House full of small children as i Have and Everything to Look after My-self. At times My Mind is so Much troubled that I Hardly no what to do with My-self. William is of no use to Me in this world, but trouble. Lavinia and Her Husband was going to Natchez and Emma Wanted to go. I thought I Had as well Let her go and take the Children and spend a little time with you as i have no one Heere to take Care of them for me & Madam I Hope it will Have the effect to rouse you spirits as i think you Need it. I Hope God will Bless us Boath to Live to see our Children a Comfort to us Boath. Emma Plays Music well and you Must Make Her a muse you & I think it will do you good.

Give my best respects to your family. Nothing More at Present.

Your friend
Jas Miller

Vicksburg Miss 24th, June 1853

Mrs Johnson

Dear Madam:

Mr Miller sent your daughter a guitar and is very anxious to know whether you got it or not.

You will please do me the favor by sending word by Mr. Knox. It was sent by Mr. Andrew Lepens and he has never let him know whether you got it or not.

Yours
Wm Henry Hicks
for M. Miller

New Orleans Aug 19th 1853

Dear Madam

I Availe My self this opertunity of writing you these few lines to inform you that I am well. Hoping that you and your family are the same. Likewise Happy to inform you that I received your Letter of the 17th inst informing Me of the good state of your Helth and Likewise that of your famely. Madame I am sory to Heere the fevour Has Broke out in your Citty for i no How the times is Heere for All kinds of Besness is stopet. My shope is doing Nothing and there is not a tenant that I Have got in My Houses that Can Pay Me one dollar rent at this time. And for the shop, I am Paying two dollars per day and Making Nothing and I am Oblige to keep it so as to Have it when I want it. I never did see the times as Bad as they are at Present. Madame if you can se Jef I think You Can send the Money By Him and Let Him give you a recept for the Amount that you give him.[1] C[h]arge Him Perticularly with it so as to Put the Letter and Money in some safe Place. Tho Madame do not distress your self By sending it if you Cant spear it handily. Madame you speak of My keeping up as i do yet Madame and I thank the Lord for that for if i was to Be taking down i do not no what whould Become of Every thing for I have no one to se to Every thing for Me. God Has Blest Me in the way of Health and Every thing Els.

Give My Best respects to your Mother and All the family.

Respectfully Your
Jas Miller

Mrs Johnson there is some Members in My family that Has very little regard for My whelfaire. More than for what they make of Me. People that
wait for ded Mens shoes gose a Long time Bare footed some times you no.

1. Jefferson Hoggatt.

New Richmond, 1853

Dear Son

I take the oppertunity of pasing upon you time of wrighting you thease
few lines that is to let you know that I have been in Bad helth all sumer, but
hoping that thease may find you and your family in good health and also
dear son I wish for you to send me some fonds for to live on through the
winter and also your sister Marthyan is having to get married in a few days
to Mr. Harris and then I will be left all alone. And also, dear son I have to
look to god for my pertecttion and you must do the same. You must not,
dear son, think that you ware left here to stay always. You must begin to
think upon the salvations of you sole and who — or — whome is he that
preaches you salvations. You must begin to think that you have to die and
after death to a Judgment. And how awful it is for one to die out of Christ
and to stand before his Judgement seat unprepared. And Know after all
that I want you to meet me, your Kind and affectionate Mother, in the
Kingdom of heaven. And also son, I would like for you to come visit this
fall to see me. The persons that you were Inquiring after I saw them two or
three times and also I wish for you to telegraph me whether you are coming
or not. Marthyan & Josephine all Joins and send their love to you and also
my compliments to Miss Johnson. My compliments to Harriet Battles and
sister, Jane Bush. And Josephine sends hers to all her little play mates and
also she is going to school and as soone as she can write she sais that she
will wright to all her play mates. And also Miss Johnson, I wish for you to
wright to me what is become of old Wm Wilie the notorious rascal for
murdering your husband and I am in hopes that the Lord will pertect you
and your little children and I am in hopes that he will pertect all in the
holer of his pertected hands. And tell sister Nancy Hilds that I am still
marching toward the promise Land and Im in hopes to meet you in the
promised Land. And also I still remains your kind and affectionate sister
untill death.

Phoebe Smith [1]

1. This letter was addressed on the back to "Missess Wm Johnson a woman of coulor, Natchez, Mississippi," and it was dated September 26, 1853. It appears to have been written to a free man of color and sent in care of Ann Johnson. By 1853 Ann was hiring free men of color to work in the barbershops constructed and previously run by her husband. Perhaps Phoebe Smith's son worked for Ann.

New Orleans March, 11th, 1855

Dear Aunt

I write you these few lines to inform you that I am just so so still complaining with my breast. It is not well yet and to say to you that you must really excuse me for not writing to you before. I must acknowledge that I do feel ashamed of myself for not writing to you before, but aunt ann I have had so much trouble since my confinement. Ann, my breast being so sore it most set me crazy. I never had so much pain in all the days of my life. I have suffered more with my breast than I did bringing the child in too the world. I have just lain for days and nights and did nothing else but cried all the time and my right breast is not well yet. It is still a running and it pains me yet once and a while it pains me and think it is the awfulest breast you ever seen. I was dressing it the other day and took down the little looking glass to look at it and upon my word my own breast frightened me. Now you may know how bad my breast looks, there is holes all over it. You may say in a manner there is five holes in it now and all of them running and it has effected my arm so that I can hardly use it. Before my breast was first lanced, I could'nt use it at all. I could'nt bear for no one to touch it. I could'nt handle the baby at all. Aunt ann, if you or mrs battles knows anything that is good for my breast I wish you would be so kind as to write me word. And as to my baby he's just the finest boy you ever looked at. He takes so much notice all of everything. He laughs all ready and trys his best to crow when you talk to him. Oh, aunt ann, about the silk, well you know the very week that you sent me the sample back to get you some like it jeff's boat did'nt get here, not until friday night. Ann, she staid here all day saturday. She didn't get away, not until sunday morning. And all day saturday I was so sick that I could'nt sit up with the back ache. Well, that very night I got up and went to the store to get the silk and the man told me that he had'nt any more, that he had sold it every bit and wanted me to take some other kind and I would'nt do it and I thought that after christmas & new years had passed then you would'nt want it. That was the reason why that I did'nt bother myself about getting any for you nor writing you word about it. It was'nt through neglect that I didn't write to you about it, nor that I did'nt get it for you. For you know aunt ann, I would do any thing for you in the world that you wanted me to get for you. And if there is anything now that you want me to get for you, just let me know and, if I can get out, I will get it for you and consider it no trouble at all.

No more at present. I remain your affectionate niece.

Emma L. Hoggatt

New Orleans April 21, 1855

Dear Aunt

I take the pleasure of writing you these few lines to inform you that i am well and all of the family except William and we expected him to die friday night. He was so low that we half to set up with him day and night. He say that he is ready to die, that god has forgiven him for all his sin he has commited. That is one thing that we rejoice in that he is ready. Friday night he shouted in his sleep. Then he told us he is ready to die. Dear aunt, i have not much to say in this letter for i feel so bad all the time.[1] Here is the hooks and eyse that you sent for and grandmother's henkercheifs. Dear aunt, i dont want you to send any money for them hooks and eyse for i have given them to you and anything that you wish me to send i will send them with the greates pleasure for you have bestow a great many things on me. Tell grandmother i will try and send her something more worthless then hankercheifs next trip or trip after next, for you and grandmother is the only friends i have. Non of the rest donnt think of me. If you pleas to tell Byron that i wrot to him and jeff never delivered the letter and that was not my fault, that he must write by the boat. Tell anna that as soon as Will get better I will write to here.

Give my love to all of my inquiring friends.

I must now bring my letter to a close by saying i remained your Dear affectionate nice un till Death. May god be with you all forever.

Octavia Miller

1. William Miller died May 6, 1855. He was twenty-five years old.

New Orleans the May 14, 1855

Dear Aunt

I write you these few lines to inform you that I received your welcome letter and I was happy to hear that you was well and also the children. I did answer your letter but the boat got broke some way another and she had to stay hear all the week. Myself and all are enjoying very good health, all but a little cold and I want you if you pleas to send me some hore hound, if you pleas. I have sent you the calico and I hope that you will be pleased with it. I am sure that it is fast collors. I gave nine cents a yard for it. It was the cheapest that I could get. I got one hundred and eleven yards for the $. The eleven yards is in the small piece. That will do for the small servants close. I hope that you will be pleased with it all. I have no news to worth your wile. Aunt, pleas dont forget to tell Cerida about the birds. I want two if I can possibly get them.

William is well. All the family sends their love to you ann and anna.

your sincer niece
Lavinia Mc Cary

Bill sends his love to you all.

New Orleans May the 20, 1855

Dear Aunt

I write you these few lines for to let you know that we are all well, hoping that these few lines may find you and all the rest of the family the same and to say to you that the reason why I did not write to you last week that I really forgot it. I was so troubled about beners going away that I forgot all about it indeed. And I am very sorry indeed to hear that lucinda is so sick. I hope that she will get better. I tell you what, aunt ann, there is so much sickness down here now the people is just dropping like flies, especially children. I thought I would of lost my baby thursday morning he was taking with such a sever cramp cholic. He just turned as pale as death and was screaming all the time just as if some one was sticking pins in him and old Mrs brustee, she's dead. She died thursday evening at four o'clock and was burried friday at six o'clock and Ann Pessie, she's dead too, and Madame fouché, Mr Nelsons wife. I was invited to the funeral, but I did'nt go. I went to old Mrs brustie's. And tell william that emma jane green is dead too. She was burried yesterday too. Well, aunt ann, I think I have wrote you all the news I think and they are very sad news indeed. Given my love to julia, mag, and all of them for me. No more at present.

I remain your affectionate neice.

Emma Hoggatt

New Orleans November the 10 55

Dear Aunt

I write you these few lines to let you know that I arrived home safe. I had a very pleasant trip of it indeed and I found them all well and stirring and they were delighted to see me indeed, but they didn't expect me that trip at all. Nor either did jeff and when I got home I found it so muddy and raining and it is still raining yet and I liked not to got out to get your dress and even now I did'nt get one like mine. They had'nt no more just like mine but I got the nearest I could get to match it and if that dont suit you aunt ann you can send it back again but I thought it was as pretty. Thats the reason why I got it and if there is any thing else, aunt ann, that you want write me word and I will get it for you and the children and all sends their love to you and father allso. I have no news to communicate to you this week. Ossy[1] sends a kiss to all of you. Tell kate and all of them how-dyedo for me. You must be sure and answer this letter and please to send me them things of mine that I left there. Give my love to eliza parker.

No more at present.

I remain your affectionate Niece
Emma Hoggatt

1. Emma and Jefferson had five children: James (who was affectionately called Ossy), Wilfred, William, Adelia, and Clara.

New Orleans April the 12, 1856

Dear Aunt

I take the pleasure of Writing you these few lines to inform you that I am quit better to What I Whare.

I Whare dreadfull all the hole Week long. I had feavor every night, but thank god that I am better. All of the rest of the family is quit well at present. I Rieceivd your Welcome letter of the 1st and Whare verry happy to here that all of the family Whare Well at present. All but grandma and I Whare verry worry indeed to heare that she Whare not Well, but I trust that she Will soon recover to her health again by the time you receive this lettter. Deare Aunt, you complain about me not Writing you a long letter.

I that present moment, I could hardly hold My pen in My hand. I know that you think that I Whare not as sick as I Writin you, but you ask Emma if I Whare sick. You see if she dont Write you the same that I did.

I feel Wright bad at this present moment so I dont think that I will be able to Wright you a long letter. You never Wright me Woard about Winston[1] and his Wife. I Would like to see them all and poor little lin and budy so much, but I hope that they are enjoying splendid health. Give My love to family and all of My inquireing and tell richard that Miss Mason has spent the day three times this Week and she send her best respect to him once again. I must really close by saying I remain your Niece

O M[2]

1. William (Bill) Winston began working for William Johnson in 1836 when he was approximately twelve years old; at that time he was a slave. His master, the former lieutenant governor of Mississippi Fountain Winston, however, freed Bill's mother, Rachel, and made provisions for Bill's freedom. Fountain Winston stated that Bill was due his freedom as he was "too white to be continued in Slavery." According to the will, Bill Winston was to be placed with "some reputable mechanic" when he was old enough to learn a trade; when he was twenty-one, he was to be freed. Fountain Winston also left Rachel his furniture and $500 as support for Rachel and Bill. The remainder of his property (which consisted of land in Tennessee worth approximately $3,000), except his library, was to be held in trust for Bill — provided that his habits continued to be good. Bill Winston was taken to Cincinnati and freed when he was twenty-one years old. He married Caroline Leaper, a free woman of color from Natchez, on March 20, 1856. Marriage Register 7-B, p. 387B, Adams County Courthouse. Fountain Winston never admitted to paternity, but the documents suggest that William was his son. For a more thorough discussion of Bill Winston, see Edwin Adams Davis and William Ransom-Hogan, *The Barber of Natchez* (Baton Rouge: Louisiana State University Press, 1974), 57–60.

2. Octavia Miller Martin.

New Orleans September the 13, 1856

Dear Aunt

I write you these few lines to let you know that we all arrived home safe and had a very pleasant trip of it indeed, but when we got home we found father quite unwell, he has been complaining ever since he came from up there and is still unwell. And Ossy, he was taken with a violent fever last night, and is quite feverly all day. And the rest of the family are all well. And I am still here yet. Don't know what time I will leave, but he came down and asked me what did I strike Herb that way for as to give him a spasm. I told him that I didn't strike him. Well no more than I didn't. I caught holt of him and told him to go long up stairs that I was going to whip him, when he fell across the steps and father says that he asked you when he was up there if I struck Herb[1] and you said yes. I will send you her letter for you to read and see what she says in it about bebe says and what you says of me just to see if you think I am deserving of all of that, but you mus'nt let no one else see you when you read it because that would raise a fuss again, because jeff got it out of his desk when he went a way for me to see it. Aunt ann will you ask cindy to look for that blue cloth of ossy's and send it to me when you send ossy's little undershirt. I have no news to write this week. Ossy keeps so sick now and cross that he won't let no one have him or nurse him but me. I commenced this letter ten o'clock this morning and finished it three o'clock this afternoon.

Now you tell julia[2] and all them the reasons why I didn't write to them but tell them I will try and write to them next week and ask julia if Sam got what I sent him to mrs mc Carys. For am [the letter is torn here] towels and ossy's shoes.

No more at present. I remain your affectionate neice,

Emma Hoggatt

1. Herb was James Miller's slave.

2. Julia and her two children, Laura, about twelve years old, and Margaret, described as an infant, were slaves who were purchased for $1,600 by Ann Johnson on June 1, 1840. Ann purchased Julia and her children so that she could free them. Since by 1840 the laws in Mississippi had changed and she could not free the slaves in the state, Ann appointed Jane Bush, who was Julia's mother and Harriett Battles's sister (and thus Jane Bush was Ann's aunt, making Julia Ann's first cousin), as the true and lawful attorney in order that they might be taken out of the state to be freed. While freeing a slave or slaves out of Mississippi was tenuous in 1840, it was the best the women could do. Some slaveholders who owned relatives chose to leave the legitimately enslaved believing they could protect them. But that solution presented its own problems. If the slaveholder died, the relatives who inherited the slaves could and sometimes did sell them. By the 1840s, for instance, Jane and her children would have been valued conservatively at approximately $1,500. The sale and power of attorney are in the William T. Johnson Collection.

New Orleans November, 1856

Dear friend

I recieved your letter with great pleasure hearin that you all are enjoying good health with exception of small complaints as we are all subject to. I for my part have been suffering since I left you with my breast. I was ordered by the Doctor to get a little dog to suck out the corrupted milk. Since then I have had the misfortune to have but one and it died two or three days afterwards for it was poisoned by the milk. And since then it is almost impossible for me to find another. Dear friend you cannot imagine how I Suffer when they [illegible text] of sweling. I have walk for days and days and it appears to me, because I want one or two I cannot find one. Specialy in a large city like this you would find it strange but it is as I tel you and witch makes it worse on me. You must know that Miss Fanny Brustee[1] has just put her brother out of doors and that we had to go and rent another house which has caused us a great trouble to moove and fix up again. I will sease this opportunity to tell you all if any of you visites our city you will find our residence in Burgundy Street, No. 334, between Bayou & Hospitale where we will be glad to meet any of you with open hand and heart if ever we meet again witch I hope will be next Summer. I have a great deal to tel you about this circumstance. Mrs. Johnson, I pray that you would see Gina's[2] father and see if he would let her comme and stay with us as I am her God mother and my husband God father. We wish both to have her! And all that a mother and a father could do we are both willing and obliged to do by the oath that we pledged to her dying mother wich we hope he will not refuse us. As for Mr McCary, he knows Gabriel to be a true friend to the family and particularly to his unfortunate deceased wife.[3] Dear friend, I have nothing of particular importance to communicate to you at prsent more then what you know by Mr J Hogatt. Give my [best] to your Mother, Grandmother, childrens and the Servants for me and tell them that my dayly thoughts is still with them as though I was amidst them all and I hope At the reception of this letter it will find you all in the same state of health as it left us.

I remain your sincere friend Victoir Brustie[4]

1. Fanny Brustee, formerly of Natchez, was the daughter of Charlotte and Gabriel Brustee. Charlotte Brustee was originally from New Orleans, Gabriel from Natchez.

2. Gina McCary, the daughter of Lavinia Miller McCary (the daughter of Adelia and James Miller) and Robert McCary Jr. (the son of Robert McCary).

3. Lavinia was killed in a steamboat explosion on the Mississippi River in 1856.

4. Victoire Brustee was the wife of Gabriel Brustee Jr., who was the son of Gabriel and Charlotte Brustee, and old friends of the Brustee family.

New Orleans December 1856

Dear Aunt

I write you these few lines to let you know that we are all well, hoping that these few lines may find you and all the rest of the family enjoying the same state of health. I received your most welcome letter and was very happy to hear from you all indeed. Ann, I was very sorry to hear that you wasn't pleased with my letter, I dont know as I put any thing in there to displeasure. I never meant to do it, but we will let that pass now. About mrs. Douce, she had, I believe, a little money that he left her and she sold a great part of his furniture that she did'nt want. And the rest she kept what she will take to furnish a smaller house with as she intends to move as soon as she can find a house to suit her at a reasonable price. And her brother the house rent for her he will pay he wants her to come live up there with him but she dont want to go, poor woman. I feel very sorry for her. She has been to see me since his death. That's all I know about it. I believe she's getting on right well. Now liz was here the other day to see me and said that Mrs Douce was coming to see me but she has'nt been yet. It has been so very cold and we have had so much rain too. It is very cold here indeed. Cold as it can be I believe. And old Mrs. Saunders is verry low. She hardly has breath in her and she is speechless. Ann, I got them shoes for you and the mireno and the black silk gloves that you wrote for. And tell sis that I tried on them shoes for her. Tell her I tried on four or five pairs and that these were the widest that they had. I had Tene[1] try on Alices and she had to get smaller ones for her. Another mireno was fifty cts a yard and the shoes were six bits a pair. You know aunt, you sent two dollars and five cts. Well, that helped to get the gloves and the mireno and I hunted for some of them little stockings for alice and Gena and I could not find any, but I will look again to see if I can find any & about the raisins — I priced them. there aint no quarter boxes and Ciffer[2] has some very large boxes for two dollars larger than common sizes. I think they are cheap. Tene got a box of them and now they are dearer than any other time. Well, I must bring my letter to a close.

No more at present. I remain your affectionate niece.

Emma Hoggatt

Give my love to them all and tell sis I hope her shoes will fit her.

1. Elenore Bingaman, the daughter of Col. Adam Lewis Bingaman, was affectionately known as Tene.

2. "Ciffer" must have been a market or marketer in New Orleans.

New Orleans January the 3, 1857

Dear Aunt

I write you these few lines to let you know that we are all well. Thank God its the beginning of a new year and I hope that these few lines may find you and all the rest of the family enjoying the same state of health. I received your letter and was very happy to hear from you all indeed, but you did'nt tell me whether you got them oranges or not that I sent you. I sent you 25 in the bag for the children, a dozen for kate, and the rest for the other children. You talk about me not writing you a word when you send me anything now you aint a bit better. I have worriness to write to you this week. We have had a great deal of rain all this week. It is awful on the clothes. I haven't seen Mrs Brustee this week yet but when I do I will tell her what you said. Tell dick[1] that his loterie ticket drew a awful large prize. That he drew more than any of us. He got a cup to drink his coffee out of in the mornings and tell him I say jeff got six cigars. I got a bottle of essence and I aint seen what tane got yet and tell him I say he could'nt write to me, but he could write to Miss Mason. Tell him never mind the mule, I will fix him for that. Tell him I say to send me my new years gift and to tell Pauline Stone and Amline[2] all howdyedo for me if he sees them.

No more at present. Give my love to all. I remain with respect your neice.

Emma Hoggatt

1. Richard Johnson, the second son of Ann and William Johnson.

2. Pauline and Emaline Stone were young friends of the Johnson and Miller women.

New Orleans March 14th, 1857

Dear Aunt

I write you these few lines to let you know that we are all well, hoping that these few lines may find you and all the rest of the family enjoying the same state of health. I received your letter and was very happy to hear from you all and you wrote me now that you did'nt receive the fifty cts. I did write you word that I put it in the letter, but jeff tole me that he would give it to you and thats the reason why that I did'nt put it in the letter, but I will be sure and put it in this time. And the reason why that I don't go to see Mrs Brustie oftener is because I know there is no necessity of it. Why, do you suppose that if I knew that she was really sick allways or that she was confined to her bed all that I would'nt go to see her. Of course, I would. I would'nt want to wait for no one to tell me to go and see her because as the old proverb goes that one good turn is all ways deserving of another. Well, now about Fannys house, you wrote to know how much she got for it. well, I believe she got fourteen hundred for it and as for me seeing her or any of them, I never do. I dont know where she lives as much and so if you was to write her a letter, I would'nt have no way in the world to send it to her. Nor would me take it myself because I dont go there. Well, I must bring my letter to a close by saying that I remain your neice.

Give my love to all.

E. Hoggatt

 ————————————————————————————

New Orleans May the 16, 1857

Dear Aunt

I write you these few lines to let you know that me and my little family is well; and I hope that this letter may find you and the rest of your family in the enjoyment of good health. You must really excuse me for not writing to you before now, but I know that when you hear my reason for not writing you wont blame me in the least. For the first week I did'nt write to you was because I was verry busy at the time finishing a dress for Maria that I had commenced for her and she wanted it for sunday. And then I was so sick that I felt more like laying down then I did like sewing and I told jeff to tell you so if any of them inquire or asked the reason for me not writing. And last week I was busy moving from the house.[1] I was drove away from it a gain all on account of Tene.[2] So you see it would of been better if I had of never went back there and now I am house keeping and Mrs Brustie boards me until I can get a servant. At first, jeff wanted me to come up there to Natchez and board with Julia. To store all my furniture as he would be doing nothing this summer and going to house keeping he said would cost so much in the summer and he would'nt be doing nothing and I was so worried and bothered that I did'nt know what to do and for a while I did think of doing it. And then I thought better of it after a while about going to Julias. I did'nt think I would be doing right as none of your family did'nt go to Julias now. And then for me to go there and stay it would'nt look right. I thought I would wait a while and acquaint you of it first and to hear what you would think and say about it. I tell you aunt Ann I was like some body standing on their head instead of their feet and Jeff he was just like a crazy man. He did'nt know what to do. He could'nt be here to do nothing for me. And being drove out of the house without a minutes warning to look for a house or nothing else. And I knew that I had to go when he told me to leave his house, to go out of his house. What was I to do. And the reason for him telling me to leave the house was for this. Last wednesday week we had a little dance at the house. Well, theres some fellow coming to see Tene by the name of Lyons, George Lyons, and he was there with his brother Felix Lyons, Jim Sanders and his wife Lenore and Jimmy, myself, Tene and Maria. We was all dancing. I was dancing with Jim Sanders and his wife was dancing with father. We was at the head of the floor and Tene was dancing with this George Lyons and Jimmy was dancing with Felix his brother. Well we was dancing our set and had'nt got through with it when Tene, she said, come ahead Mr Lyons its our turn. And I seen by the looks of Lyons then that he did'nt look pleased and him and Tene cuts right across the floor and in coming back again I was watching him. He elbows his self as much to say get out of my way and all most knocks me down and I turns around and says to him: why Mr Lyons, I am astonished at you. When he pretends to excuse himself when if I had'nt of seen with what intentions he did it whist I might of excused him but I did'nt do it, and from that it commenced. Tene she cries and carries some ridiculous about that man why she could'nt of done worse than if she had been engaged to him. And i told her so. And father, he says to me: well, did'nt you do so about Jeff. Now, as if Tene was engaged to this fellow and father dont know more about him nor his caracter than you do. And there he comes and sits until twelve o'clock at night and father is never the man to go in there once all will be gone to bed in the house but them two. And as soon as Tene knows that that man's boats in and he dont come to the house she dresses herself and goes to see him and before she was acquainted with this man a month she went and gave him a daguerratype. Well, now you know aunt Ann that aint right for nobody to do. Oh, I have'nt time to tell you one half. I expected to come up there this week on some business maybe I will come up next week if I can make all appointments. No more at present. Give my love to all.

I remain with respect
Emma Hoggatt

1. During those early years of her marriage, Emma and Jeff Hoggatt and their children lived in the house with her father, James Miller. Jeff was a barber working on steamboats that traveled up and down the river; thus he was frequently away from home.

2. Verene Miller, Emma's sister.

New Orleans July 11th, 1857

Dear Aunt

I write you these few lines to let you know that we are all well or at least we are just tolerable for I am not well nor Ossy for he has got the bad dysentery from eating so many figs. But I hope that these few lines may find you better than it leaves me and I am very sorry to hear of the death of old aunt diaz. Aunt ann, she did'nt have time to prepare herself or nothing at all poor old thing. Aunt Ann, aunt Ann, aunt Ann, you must not think hard of what I said in my letter for I meant no harm what ever and I dont want you to think so either. Now for me to tell you about a woman that jeff bought today. She seems to be a woman very willing. Says she can make homemade bread, buscuits, pies and do everythin thats wanting about the house and if she suits I will be just fixed wich I hope she will. I am in a hurry and aint got much time to say much and aunt Ann tell sis that I aint got time to write her this week and if sis sees Pauline that I will write to her another time. I liked to forget about them apples. I am a thousand times oblige to you for them indeed. I must close my letter. No more at present. I remain your affectionate neice.

E Hoggatt

New Orleans the 14th Febr 1858

Kind Mdm

I received your letter last night after waiting on the warf in the cold and rain until twelve o'clock in ful expectation of incircling in my arms my long lost wife, but was Struck with horror to having been so disappointed. I have been nourishing in my heart since my last letter to you and her thousands of good feelings and building up castles that we may meet again and live happy together until it will please God to separate us by Death and hope still to live together in soul in the next world. I wrote my wife to come the last trip on particular bussiness. I dont now weather she told you about that or not but I will. The lot that she owns is about to be seised and being that she is not here the person that has the note waited for her last trip and was very much vexed to see that she did not come. I had to go and see him and tell him that my wife would have been here this trip but was unable to come on account of sickness, but positively that she would be here this coming fryday and he again give me until then. Victoir[1] must not take for excuse that she has no money as she told to her sister-in-law. For she [k]now full well that I would see that her passage would be paid and that is no excuse. I beg you to talk to her and make her see that this is no time to neglect buissiness that concernes her for she knows that the propertie is on her name and that she alone can arrange this buissiness with that man. Although, he say that he must sell, but if my wife come he will let her sell it her self. Therefore, you see I cannot sell nor seign any papers wateaver and if she dont come he will put it up at public auction. So you see it is best for her to come and try to sell it privately for she will get more for it. And again, I have been waiting for her the last six weeks for me to get a convinient house for us that I might start a shop and live happy with her and my son in the same house and I would be working outdoors she would always be there to answer when any work should come in. So you see that I am placed in a situation that I cannot do one thing nor the other for if I take a small shop I will have two rents to pay and that will not do. By taking one that I can work and live in, it will be best for us and the balance of the money that may remain Ernest and myself can work together and perhaps accumulate more than what the lot is worth. I speak to her and his advantage and I have no doubt but that you see yourself that my intentions are good and am confident if I had my wife her[e] and could talk to her personnelly she would see for herself. For conversing together privately and writing letters makes a great differents between husban and wife. Therefore, she must not miss this trip as I shall be waiting for her until the boat arrives. I have nothing more to say at present but to returne you my sincere thanks for all that you have done and still will do in reconciliating me and my wife. And I shall never in this world forget your kind feelings in our little Difficulties wich I hope is almost come to an end as I said before all depends on my wife. My doors are always & will always be opened for her or my son; although, he has disobeyed me in my orders to him. But if his mother still persist for him to stay, she may use her one discretion as to that for I dont wish to act against her will. But, at the same time, I [k]now that it is very wrong in so doing for he would be a great help to me being that he [k]nows already how to work in our bussiness and take my interest and his mothers. But it is no us[e]. As my wife will have her own way and I must adhere to all that she wants.

Please give my respect to all the family, Mrs McCary, and also accept the same.

I remain your friend and humble
Mr G Brustie[2]

1. Victoire Brustee.
2. Gabriel Brustie Jr., the son of Charlotte and Gabriel Brustee.

New Orleans February the 14, 1858
Dear Aunt

I write you these few lines to let you know that we are all well, hoping that these few lines may find you and the rest of the family enjoying the same state of health and to let you know that I received your most welcome letter and was very happy to hear from you all. I have got the cotton and shoes for you wich you sent for. It is not quite as wide as the pieces you get, but it was the widest he had and he promised to send it in an hours time, but he has'nt sent it yet. And I dont know if he will send it now in time for jeff to take it with him. I have no news to write you this week. They are all busy fixing for to go to the ball to night and turning the house upside down with their fixings and they are all going a gain monday to a fancy dress ball, Marday gras as the French people call it, all dressed in costumes. It is so dreadful warm to be dancing to night its enough to make one faint. And friday night such a rain we had you never seen. It was a perfect river here all over the banquets and it is constantly rain here. We seldom have any dry weather here now and it rains all the time. I have no more to say. I must bring my letter to a close. No more at present. I remain with respect

E. Hoggatt

New Orleans April 10th 1858
Dear Aunt

I write you these few lines to let you know that we are all just tolerable, for I cant say well, for we are not, for Ossy, he has got the mumps. And the baby he is not quite well of the thrush yet and for myself I have a bad cold and so you see there is none of us well. But I hope that these few lines may find you and the rest of your family enjoying better health than what I am just now. I received your most welcom letter and I was very happy to hear from you indeed and I was very sorry to hear of you feeling so sad when you wrote me word. I felt so myself. There was a man hung here on friday for killing his mistress in october last. The papers states he got religion before he died and when he was in his cell just before he was to be hung he was praying and singing at such a rate that every one present was shocked at the way he put up such a fervent prayer and sang such a beautiful hymn and they had two ministers there with him and he died very happy indeed. No more at present. Give my love to all. I remain with respect.

E. Hoggatt

Aunt Ann, I expect I will christen the baby next week and dick[1] is going to stand god father for him and he told me to tell sis to make some cakes and to send them to him sure next week. I wish sis and kate could come down to the christening, but I know that it is just as hard to move them as it is to move you, so you must excuse this letter. No more at present. I remain with respect

E Hoggatt

1. Richard Johnson.

 _____

New Orleans June 19 1858

Dear friend

I write you these few lines to let you know that we are all well, hoping that these few lines may find you and all the rest of the family enjoying the same state of health. The linen that you told me [to] price for you prices some at seven dollars, some at eight, some at nine, and some at fifteen dollars, and the head handkerchiefs that you told me to get for you at twenty cts a piece, I could not get them less than twenty five cents a piece. This week I have been sick. I had the fever, but I am better now. And tell Anna that I did'nt send her the herbs because I couldn't get them. I did not write to you because I thought Jeff wasnt going a way was the reason why I did'nt write. I have no more news to write you this trip. Ma and all of them sends their love to Jim. Give my respect to Mrs McCary and to Mrs battles. No more at present. I remain your sincere friend.

Victoire Brustie

New Orleans June 26th 1858

Dear friend

I write you these few lines to let you know that all of the family are well, hoping that these few lines may find you and all the rest of the family enjoying the same state of health.

I have sent you the dresses that you sent to me for fourteen yards in each piece and the shoes for you. It all came to four dallars and seven dimes. And I heard that Man[1] was sick, but I hope that by the time that you receive this letter he will be better. I didnt get the linnen for you be cause I didnt think it will be thick enough for mens shirts but if you want it for chemises, I think it will do. And in the bundle that I have sent, you will find some samples and they are all fifteen cents a yard. Them herbs, I sent them to Anna and to ask her if they are the right kind and if they are not to send me more and I will get the kind. The money that you sent last week was just what it cost or the things cost. I have no more news to write to you this week, only that they have commenced to seize the old mans things, my old uncle.

Give my love to all of the family. And ma and all of them sends their love to you. No more at present. I remain your sincere friend.

V. Brustie

1. Clarence, the youngest son of Ann and William Johnson, was affectionately called "Man," or "the little man."

New Orleans August 7th 1858

Dear Aunt

I write you these few lines to let you know that we are all well, hoping that these few lines may find you and the rest of your family enjoying the same state of health. I received your letter and I was very happy to hear from you all indeed. And I received the money that you sent me. Allso two dollars. And for the muslin that you told me to let emline get for you, She could'nt find any no wheres at that price. Being that the summer seasens are all most over now they have sold out the whole stock of cheap muslins. You did'nt tell me what you wanted for your self or the children. One man he had some green, but the green allways fade and she would'nt get that. I have no news to write to you this week. It is very dusty here now indeed.

We have'nt had any rain here now for some time. And hot, its just hot enough for to melt a brass monkey. You did'nt write me word how much them peaches that you sent me cost. You tell me how much they cost and I would pay you. No more at present. I remain, with respect.

Emma Hoggatt

Old Alsina is down here staying at old Louis Wileys.[1]

1. A friend of the family.

Natchez August 27, 1858

Mrs. Johnson

Madam

I have a Chance to buy 10 Bales Hay at One Dollar per Bale. Send me word as quick as possible if you want it.

Your obt Servant

Jas. Johnson

New Orleans December 11, 1858

Dear Aunt

I write you these few lines to let you know that we are all well, hoping that these few lines may find you and the rest of your family enjoying the same state of health. I received your letter and was very happy to hear from you all indeed and to let you know that I wrote to you week before last and jeff he brought the letter back again because the boat didnt get there not untill twelve o'clock at night and coming down she didnt get there untill it was late, and he said he didnt see anyone at that time a night and thats the reason why you didnt get my letter. I have no news to write to you this week we have had some very cold weather here indeed and to day soon we have rain and it makes the weather bad and muddy. Charlotte[1] and Pauline has been here to see me since they came back and Charlotte had more talk than enough and what she didnt talk about is what she did not know. And she asked me about Tene and what kind of a place was that where she stays at. And Ann, every thing else. And I just told her what I knew about it and no more. And Jeff met Tene and Pauline in the street together. I dont know weather she is going to stay at Ellens or go back to stay with Mary. I haven't seen any of them since she's been sick. I must hurry my letter to a close. I have no more news. I have sent you these shoes.

No more at present. I remain with respect. Oh, Em told me to tell Erma that that she will writ next week.

E H [2]

1. The daughter of Mary Williams Bingaman and Adam Lewis Bingaman. Adam Bingaman was an influential white man in Natchez. Mary Williams was a free woman of color. The couple must have moved to New Orleans by 1866 as their son, James Bingaman, died there in that year. Adam Bingaman officially acknowledged his racially mixed son in the probate records. See Records of Notary Public, Edward D. Godchald, July 13, 1865, New Orleans, Louisiana.

2. Emma Hoggatt.

New Orleans June 25, 1859

Dear Mother

It is with pleasure that i adress you those few lines to let you know that we are well and hope that those few lines may find you and all of the family in the same state of good health. Ma, i received those things that you sent me and i more than oblight to you for them, but i would have bin a great els more pleased if you had of sent me some money to. I have got a pair of shoes with as i stand a great deal in need of them at present. There is no work to be got at present. Jeff will tell you the same. All the large houses are nearly much closed. There is Bub Brustie who bin out off work for very long time and can not get any to do. I was about to go on the steamer Morning Light up Red River and she had shuch a few passengers on board that i gave it up and i whent so far as to fix the shop up for nothing. I have had the offer off a jobs on the Lacomport. She is a lake boat, but i would not accept it because i could not make anything unless I kept a card table and i could not set up so much at might so i gave it up. Ma, i wish you would send me five Dollars. I stand in very much need of it. I have got 6 pair off pantaloons and 3 or 4 coats. At the present i stand much in need shoes at prersent i have had but two pair off shose. Since i came down the first pair lasted long than any i have ever had in my life. If i can get in an kind off work i am going at it. I think i go up red river next trip. Ma you must excuse this bad leter. Give my love to all of the family. I must end my leter by saying remain your afectionate son.

Richard M. Johnson [1]

1. Richard Johnson, like Jefferson Hoggatt and many other free men of color, worked as barbers on the steamboats that traveled up and down the Mississippi River, but as this letter attests, the work was scarce, and the men and women often lived in poverty.

New Orleans July 23, 1859

Dear Mother

It is with pleasure I adress you Those few lines to let you know that i am well and I hope that those few lines may find you and all of the family in the same State of health. Ma, i wish you had of seen how i waded in to the cucumbers and the Cabage. I eat untill I like to busted. Ma, I wish you tell sis to send me my book called Poetry and Prose of europe and america and lend me some of her Books to read and tell Lucinda I have sent her the cage and i will be very much Obliged to her for the bird and emma says she will be the same. Tell Sis, Em[1] says she will write next trip and my two Sisters, Pinky and Lizz Douce, send their love to you and Sis and Cate.[2] They Call me brother all the time so i have some sisters down here two. Emma says she is very much Obliged to you for the peaches and i am more than Obliged to you for the vegetables and thank jim[3] two for me.

Ma, i stand very much in need of a hat at present.

Ma i will write more next trip. Give my love to all of the family.

No more at present. I remain your affectionate son.

Richard M Johnson

1. Emma Hoggatt.
2. Sis and Cate are Anna and Catherine.
3. One of the family's slaves.

New Orleans October 1, 1859

Dear Aunt

I write you these few lines to let you know that we are all well, at present, hoping, that these few lines may find you and the rest of your family enjoying the same state of health, and to say to you that I received your most welcomed letter & I was very happy to hear from you all. I have no means to communicate to you this week. It is very windy and dusty down here indeed and mostly every one is out of water. I have sent you your dress at last. Thank god I felt well enough for to go out and get it for you this week and I hope that you will be pleased [with] it for it suits my taste and my fancy better than the other one for you. And I have sent you buddys shoes too. Such shoes as them costs one dollar and six bits apair. And the calico that was twenty five cents a yard. I hope you wont think it is too much. I think that is all that I have to say. Oh no, about the soap. The reason why that I have'nt sent you your soap before now was because Jeff told me that he could get it for down to the steamboat better and handier than what I could by buying it along the streets and let the man put it right aboard for him. I have been waiting on him all this time and every time he comes and I ask him about it he tells me that he forgot it. It is not my fault that you have not got your soap before now. It is all his fault, and now he says that he will get it next week for you. No more at present. I remain with respect.

E. Hoggatt

New Orleans April 21st 1860

Mrs Johnson

I write you to inform you of the marriage of my daughter, Marie, Sophie Charlotte Bingaman, to St. Felix Cazanave. She will be married at the St Louis Cathedral, on the evening of the 30th April. As we will have but a family wedding, we have issued no invitations, but we will send your family a piece of her wedding cake. We are all well, and hope that you are all the same; the children join me in love to you all.

Yours respectfully

M. E. Bingaman[1]

1. Mary E. Williams Bingaman was a free woman of color who had grown up outside of Natchez. As an adult, she was involved in a liaison with the white colonel Adam Lewis Bingaman. This letter discreetly announces the marriage of their daughter, Charlotte, known as "Teen." Before moving to New Orleans with Mary Williams, Adam Bingaman had been one of Natchez's most distinguished citizens. He was born near the city in 1793. He graduated from Harvard as the "first scholar of his class" in 1812. By 1819 Bingaman had become a planter, and between 1819 and 1841, he inherited much of the property that had previously belonged to his family. At one point he owned several plantations around Natchez and 235 slaves. He served in the War of 1812 and in the Natchez Militia. During the 1830s and 1840s, he was a leader of the Whig Party in Mississippi. By 1850, Adam Bingaman had moved to New Orleans with Mary and their children, Charlotte, Elenore.

Bolivar County September 7th 1862

Miss Cattrinne Johnston[1]

As [Priest Hodge] leave here tomorrow for Natchez, I will favor you with a few lines. I am glad to inform you that I arrived here safe on Thursday evening — and I am *well*. I found our Reg't about 10 miles from the Miss

River in the swamp — but the health seemed to be very good among the *men.*[2] We are in Bolivar Co. opposite Arkansas. It is a very pretty county up here & some very pretty streams. The Bogue Falaya on which we are now camped is a beautiful stream, about 50 yards wide & perfectly clear, fine fishing. And when we are not engaged with the Yankees we pass off the time in fishing. As I have just arrived I have not much news of importance to write you. Please write to me on the return of Col Hodgatt. Let me know how Richard is getting. I hope he has recovered. My love to all the family — also to Miss Anna Miller. Miss Anna, I will write to Miss Anna at the first opportunity. I wrote to Anthony.[3] Give your letters to him I will be sure to get them. My best regards to all the family. I would like to hear from your GrandMother.

Yrs Very Respectfully
William Hoggett[4]

1. This is the first time the family name is spelled "Johnston."

2. It is not clear which regiment William Hoggatt joined. It is interesting to note that it would have been a regiment of free men of color, and it was probably one from New Orleans as several were formed there.

3. An apprentice to William Johnson.

4. During his youth, William Hoggatt was also an apprentice to William Johnson.

Natchez, Nov the 8th 1863

Dear Friend[1]

I suppose you will be some what surprised at receiving a letter from me after my long silence, but believe me though I have not written to you I have not forgoten you. I have promised myself over and over to write to you, but somehow I could not commence. I took out my paper to write to you last week, but had to stop to attend to some thing else. I wrote you a long letter a good while ago to which I never received any answer. It is very dul up here. There appears to be nothing doing in any business. Eugenia[2] sends her love to you & says that you can send up the comfort you said you wanted her to fix for you and she will try & do it for you. You ought to see Gena now she is just as fat as she can be. She looks like an Irish girl. She was telling me that you wanted her to persuade Grand Ma to move to New Orleans to live. My goodness! it would take a fortune to move us any where. There is so many of us and another thing, I dont believe any thing would induce Grand Ma to leave Natchez. She has been complaining a good deal lately of pains in her limbs & she allows herself to be worried so easily, but she does very well to be as old as she is. We have had some few cases of Yellow Fever & other Fevers up here this summer, but Thank God, our family have kept healthy. Dear friend, I wish you would be so kind as to go and see poor William for me & let me know how he is. I have no news to write you of any interest at present. Give my love to your Mother & Sisters when you see them. Grand Ma and all the family join me in love to your self and family, hoping to hear from you soon. I am as Ever

Your Sincere Friend
Anna L. Johnson

1. This letter was addressed to Victoire Brustie.
2. The youngest daughter of Ann Battles Johnson and William T. Johnson.

*Anna L. Johnson, the daughter of Ann Battles Johnson and William Johnson, c. 1880,
Natchez, Mississippi. (Courtesy of Dr. Thomas H. Gandy, Natchez, Mississippi)*

Certificate of Baptism, drawn from the Third Book, in which are written the Baptisms of free persons of Colour, of the Cathedral and Parrochial Church of St Louis, of this City and Parish of New Orleans, in the State of Louisiana, United States of America.

Ann
Johnson
and
Battles,
a legitimate child

In the year of our Lord, one thousand eight hundred and forty two, and on Wednesday, the twentieth instant of the month of July: I, the undersigned, Edmond D'hauw, Priest and Vicar of the Cathedral and Parrochial Church of St Louis of this City and Parish of New Orleans, in the State of Louisiana, United States of America: solemnly baptized Ann Johnson, born in this aforesaid Parish, on Tuesday, the twenty fifth instant of the month of March of last year, one thousand eight hundred and forty one; a legitimate daughter of William Johnson, and of Ann Battles his consort, both of them natives of the City of Natchez, State of Mississippi, in the aforesaid United States of America, in which place they are residing. Stood as Godfather and Godmother, Lewis Delorgne, and Linnia Miller.

In Testimony whereof I have signed.

(Signed), C. D'hauw.

I the undersigned, do hereby certify the foregoing to be a true and faithful Copy of the Original Act, Kept in the Records of the aforesaid Church under my charge, Goo redress.

New Orleans July 25th 1842.

B. Mbohringer Priest & ad beli cure

The baptism record of Anna L. Johnson. (William T. Johnson Collection, by permission of Hill Memorial Library, Louisiana State University)

OATH OF ALLEGIANCE TO THE UNITED STATES.

[See President's Proclamation, December 8, 1863.]

I, *Mrs. Anna Johnson* .... do solemnly swear in the presence of Almighty God, that I will bear true allegiance to the United States, and defend the same, and will henceforth faithfully support, protect and defend the Constitution of the United States, and the Union of the States thereunder, and that I will in like manner abide by, and faithfully support all acts of Congress passed during the existing rebellion with reference to slaves, so long and so far as not yet repealed, modified or held void by Congress, or by decision of the Supreme Court; and that I will in like manner faithfully abide by and support all proclamations of the President made during the existing rebellion having reference to slaves, so long and so far as not modified or declared void by decision of the Supreme Court—So HELP ME GOD.

Sworn to and subscribed before me at my office
in *Natchez, Miss.*, this...*27*..day of
..*Dec*...............A. D., 186

Anna Johnson

J. J. Bechtel
Lieut. and Provost Marshal.

DESCRIPTION.

Name, *Anna Johnson*
Height, *5 feet 4 in.*
Eyes, *Black*
Occupation,

Age, *45*
Complexion, *Dark*
Hair, *Black*
Residence, *Natchez*

Nativity *Miss.*

The oath of allegiance to the United States that Ann Battles Johnson, like other southern slaveholders, was required to sign. (William T. Johnson Collection, by permission of Hill Memorial Library, Louisiana State University)

New Orleans november the 21st

Dear Aunt

I write you these few lines to inform you that I received your welcom letter and was happy to hear that your self and family is inj[o]ying good health as these few lines now leaves myself and sisters and brothers and cathrien is very well and is going now to mary jordans house to play Ellen was hear yesterday and spent the evening with us. I received the dress and apron and nyght gown for cathrien and the pepper and I am very much obliege to you. I have sent the little shaw[l] up by jeff I had not time to go out to get the calico but I will send it next trip. kate sends her love to all the children. give my love to william and all the children emma had not time to write you this trip kiss joe for me and alice. give my love to your ma. jeff is waiting for my letter if you se julia tell her that I had not time to answer her letter but will answer it next week I heard mag was to be marred to bill hoggett is it true. I must stop.

no more at present I remain your sincer neice Lavinia Miller you aught to of broke old Mrs coalmians neck out of your

A letter from Lavinia Miller, daughter of Adelia Johnson Miller and James Miller, to Ann Battles Johnson. (William T. Johnson Collection, by permission of Hill Memorial Library, Louisiana State University)

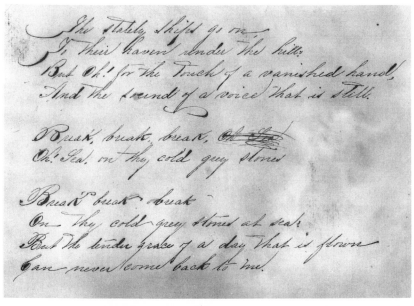

Entries from 1851 in the household account book of Ann Battles Johnson. (William T. Johnson Collection, by permission of Hill Memorial Library, Louisiana State University)

A poem written by Catharine Johnson. (William T. Johnson Collection, by permission of Hill Memorial Library, Louisiana State University)

The house on State Street in Natchez, where the Johnson-Miller women lived. Today it is owned by the National Park Service; they plan to turn the house into a museum. (Thomas H. Gandy and Joan W. Gandy Collection © 1997)

The Postwar Family Letters
of the Johnson-Miller Women
of Natchez *and* New Orleans

New Orleans July 11, 1864

Mrs Battles

I am happy to inform you that i received your welcome letter of 9thinst[1] informing Me of the good Health of your self and famely and i am Happy to inform you that we are All in good Health at Present tho i Have Been quite sick for some time My self tho i am Better at Present. Mrs Battles you wish to no of Me a Bout your Bissness & William Johnson's Where at Enny time that Mr Johnson toald Me that you Made the first Payment on the Property on Main street for He Had no Money and i will swhere to it that i will avale you Everything. Mrs Battles the times Has Been quite Harde with Me for some times. I Have Lost so Much By rents of My Houses and the Heavy tax that ive Had to Pay on Property and the rents are Low what they where and Hard to get at that.

Nothing more at Present. Give My Best respects to All the family

respectfully yours & soforth

Jas Miller

1. "9thinst" probably means "19."

Bruinsburg August 24th, 66

I have this moment received a letter from Mary informing me of your great affliction. I lose not a moment, Harriett, to express to you my heartfelt sympathies in this your great bereavement. I know how sad, how bitter, the trial. How hard to submit the loss of a loved child & that an only daughter.[1] Most truly & most sincerely I feel for you & with you my friend for I have passed through the same. Would I could comfort you in your great greef.[2] [illegible text] is your consolation time of relief. God in his infinite wisdom knows what is best. I [illegible text] to be reconciled. Do not grieve to much. You will ruin your health & unfit your duties which are before you. Your heavenly Father has taken Poor Anne from you & her family & left *you*. Believe & trust that in wisdom he has done it all. You know how Anne leaned upon & looked up to you as her main stay & had you been removed from her, how she would have suffered & how lost she would have been. I write this to you Harriett to cause you to feel that you have been left for a purpose & we know that the Almighty does not willingly afflict or grieve his children. You have *her* children. May you be a source of comfort & consolation to them. They owe you much & may you all comfort one another. Do you not think that it is best that Anne was taken & you left. I live with [illegible text] as hard as it may be. Full [illegible text]. I know the struggle to be [illegible text]. Look then my kind friend for [illegible text] been one to me in suffering, & affliction & trial. [illegible text] from whence all consolation flows & strive to feel. You cannot say "Thy will be done." I feel how inadequate words are to bring comfort to your wounded spirit. But it may be some gratification & comfort to know how deeply I feel & sympathize with you. I wish much I could see you at this time, but I fear to leave him on account of sickness, but later in the season I trust I will see you & find you more reconciled until then Harriett stive to be so & take care of your health for your grandchildren's sake & for those who care for you. You may be assured that Mary & my self feel no little affection for you. I would give much if Jim could be with me. Give my love to the Children & tell Anna I shall be glad to get a letter from her. To let me know how you are & how getting along. & with assurances of sympathy & affection. Believe me yr friend.

Anna de N. Evans[3]

1. Ann Battles Johnson died in August, 1866.
2. This letter is badly deteriorated.
3. Probably the wife of Thomas Evans, a longtime neighbor of Ann and William Johnson.

New Orleans December 6, 1867

Dear Cousin[1]

It affords me great pleasure to Inform you that I have this day Received from the persons which you Sent Me a Bag of Walnuts & C. for Which I return my Sincere thanks. And Which gives Substantial prove that you had not forgotten your promise. And I am more than pleased with the Present. You will please remember My Most Sincere regards, Love, & best Wishes to the family hoping these few lines May find you and the family enjoying good health. Theophile[2] also sends a Kiss for you all. Theodore sends his best Respects to the family & wishes you much prosperity.

Dear Cousin, I would Send you Some "Oysters," but owing to the Weather so Warm and irregular. I will not attempt to Send You any until the Weather is More Better And gets Cold. Hoping these few lines May find You and the family as it now leaves me in good health.

> I beg leave to Remain
> Respectfully Your affectionate
> Cousin
> Octavia Martin
> 349 Bienville St.

1. Byron Johnson.
2. The son of Octavia Miller Martin and Theodore Martin.

 ────────────────────────────────

TO Miss Anna L. Johnson

New Orleans Sept. 18th 1868

Dear Miss

I cannot have the least objection to your taking your cows from among my stock & if you will send out, they will be cheerfully returned. I did not know of it or I would have informed you of it. The young ladies are very well & at a surprise party to night. I have not seen William lately. But I know he is well as I required to the Keeper of the Asylum to let me know when he was unwell. Your blackberry jam is excellent & I am much obliged for it. The girls join me in love to you & your family.

> With the greatest regard
> Yours as ever
> A.L. Bingaman

 ────────────────────────────────

St. Genevieve September 21st 1868

Dear Sister

If there is any letter from me please send them down by Spencer. The worms have cleaned me out effectually & white Bet got in to the Peanut Patch last evening and tried to clean me out. Then also coming down last night, the tyre ran off the front wheel of the Buggy just above Blacks gate and I had to run the buggy in his lot and foot it from there home. Tell Juanito to go to Danemans and get a jack and send me down a bar of soap. Send Spenser down as soon as possible.

> From Your Brother
> Byron [1]

1. Byron leased Carthage Plantation near Natchez in 1868. He sharecropped it with several families.

New Orleans Nov. 12 1868

Anna

I am More than sorry to hear that Yourself & family is not enjoying good health, but I hope that this letter may find you all enjoying good health. As to My health, I Cannot boast for I am at this present time somewhat pretty ill. Remember My sincere regards, respects, & best Wishes to all the family. And tell Grandma that I sympathae with her and is very sorry to hear of her illnes. I Received your letter & the money enclosed to purchase shoes for you. You May rest assured dear Cousin that there is no trouble in it. And furthermore, I more than allways ready & willing to confer a favor whenever it is required. I forward your shoes in care of Mrs. Amos Moss & also this letter. It is the best pair that I could find for the price. The times have been very frightful in this City for the past few days, but at present everything is quiet. I am painful to hear that Gina has had the same attack, but May God grant that it never again occur. Remember My love once more to the family & also Bill McCary & family & tell him to kiss all the children & Please, dear Cousin, tell Sara to send My potatoes by M. Amos Moss on the steamer Wild Wagoner & for which I will ever remain thankful. As to the quilt pieces as spoken of in your letter, dear Cousin as I have never purchased any, you will please have the kindness to send me a sample and as I have had no opportunity of going out lately owing to my illness it is impossible for me to know what kind to purchase. But upon the receipt of the sample I will immediately comply with your request.

Believe me to be truly as ever your
affectionate Cousin
Octavia Martin
352 Conti Street

Tell Kate — that her love — is allways Accepted — "if she remembers me" — give her My love —

New Orleans December 16th 1868

Dear Miss Anna,

I send you by the Waggoner a bbl of sugar & one on flour, according to the bill of sale herewith enclosed. I hope that you may find them both good.

If there is any fault send them back. I saw William day before yesterday. He looks a little slim but is in good health. He appeared gladly pleased with your shirts. Teen[1] and Pauline are very well and in town today. They request me to give you their love & to the family.

I am doing very well in health but not otherwise. My regards to You & to Miss Gina[2] and all the family.

Yours Resp
A.L. Bingaman

1. Verene Miller.
2. Eugenia Johnson.

New Orleans February 9 1869

Dear Anna

With the greatest of pleasure I will endeavor to answer your kind letter which came saf to hand and indeed was sorry to hear that you were disappointed. The next day i went right away to find out where Col. A.L. Bingaman lived and Mrs. J. Hoggett[1] told me to go to Miss Stevanna Elicott and give her the letter that she would send it right away to Col A. L. Bingaman. That she knowed wher he lived that she could not direct me where he lived and i asked Miss Stevanna Elicott[2] to send the letter right away and she said she would as i told her it was a letter of importance business. And i have proofed that i did deliver the letter to Stevanna Elicott and think it was verry mean in her to serve me such a low act as that. Col. A.L. Bingaman and Miss Teen and Miss Pauline Ellicott[3] all were here and the Col has the box and it has been a waiting for him to come after it and he has got it. But i suppose that the cake is unfit for him to eat. As i done as i was directed by Mrs J. Hoggett and could not do any more. I have brought letters and bundles and packages before today and never has had any trouble before now and always deliverd them. But i am sorry to my heart that you had missed the boat and Mr J Hoggett did not get it for i felt miserable under this. But i done exactly as i was directed by Mrs J Hoggett and could not do any more. My best love to all of the familey and yourself, that is if it is exceptible and Mother [sends] love to all of the family. Her boat will be in tomorrow evening and i shall endeavor to inform her about how Miss Stevanna Ellicott served me. I have give all the satisfaction any person can give. You will oblige me verry kindly to answer this letter immediately. That is, if it is exceptible.

I remain Your Devoted
Friend if i am consider that

Direct your letters in care of Mr William Johnson. It was the writing and spelling.

Stevanna Payne

1. Emma Hoggett.

2. Probably a daughter of St. John Ellicott, one of Natchez's influential white planters.

3. The daughter of St. John Ellicott and Stevanna's sister.

 ——————————————————————————————————

New Orleans March 9th, 1869

Dear Anna

With the greatest of pleasure, i will endeavor to answer your ever welcome letter which came safe to me and i hope that these few lines may find you and all the family in good health as these few lines leaves me and my Mother enjoying the same good health at the present time. Dear friend, you say that you was sorry that i was put to so much trouble. It was not any trouble to me. It was my heart delight to delivred the letter and allso the box, but after you written to me that Miss Teen written to you that she had not received neither the letter nor the box, if i had of been me in Miss Teen place no sooner than i received a letter from you i would went out and enquired about the letter and box and where it was and got it before i would set myself down and wrote to you stating i had never received the letter nor the box. She should of put herself to little trouble. I suppose it was to much trouble for her do so, but certain if I had of been in her place and anything directed my father care i would found where the person was and allso got the things and if it had nott of been the respects i had for you and her father i would of written her a note to give her understanding who i was. It is true i am poor but i am proud and i hope that I have the pleasure of seeing Miss Teen and then I simple give her a few remarks but I hope by me saying what i have said about Miss Teen it will not break up our corresponding with each other. If it do i can not help. My love to all the family if it is exceptible. I herd that Josephine Nicks[1] is married to Mr. William Holsom. Is it true? She was engage to him before i left. Write me all the news. The firemans turn out here on the fourth of March. They look beautifull, but it was not such a pretty day. They had showers of rain, but they did not mind it and had a verry bad night of it. Times are very gay down here to me, but person says that stays here says times is dull, but the times do not seems dull to me. My respects to Mr Warner and his brother, that is if exceptible. Excuse the writing and blots of ink as Mr Johnson is waiting. Nothing more at present. Please answer Mother. Love to all the family. Please answer my letter and receive for yourself a Sincere friends. Love to you

From Your Devoted Friend
Stevanna Payne

1. Josephine Nix, the daughter of William Nix, a free man of color who had been an apprentice to William Johnson.

Natchez Miss. May 15th 1871

Miss Anna,

I take the opportunity to write you a few lines to let you know that I am well and I hope this letter may find you the same. I will bring your books home some evening this week. I can't bring them in the mornings when I come to school because they are to heavy. I cant bring them this evening because sisy is coming to see me. I forgot to bring my little book. This letter will do for to day. Wont it? Miss Anna, i dont want that book what you promised me till friday. I take good care of it. I could not get you a pretty boquet this morning because it was lat.

I remain you
sincere little friend
Meedora [1]

1. This letter appears to be from one of Anna Johnson's students.

Miss A L Johnson Natchez Miss.

Black Lake Plantation May 31, 1872

Dear Sister

I write you those few lines to In form you that I am well and geting a long quite well, thank god. The Crops are looking very well, as well as any Crops I have seen and I have seen right sharp of them a round a bout here. I have sent the waggon in to move Patience things in. Her and Jack has fallen out and it is jest as well that they have for his family is all the help he requires. The out side crop question has a gain been brought up and dis posed off. I hope to the satisfaction of all partis. I have give the hands the privlege of taking in all land not now in cultivation, giving you the half off all crops raised there on whitch I believe has caused a general satisfatction.

Sis, I wish you would look over the books and See if Richard O' Coner is credited with 5 days work done in George Corks squad last year. I my self know that he worked there 5 days. Sis, Please try an send me out a sack of oats and corn if you can. Do not send yellow corn. Please. And send me out them peas you told me you would try to get for me. White peas, I want 3 or 4 pints. I want tell Jim to please send me that plow Beam on the shed in the loft. Ann look up the kitchin stairs and send me the box off waggon grease up there.

Your Brother

Richard M. Johnson [1]

1. Richard Johnson had been diagnosed with valvular heart disease at some point before 1865. The diagnosis was noted on his exemption from service in the Black Mississippi Militia, but he had evidently recovered from his heart disease by 1872 because he was running Black Lake Plantation in that year. The people he mentions in this letter worked the farm with him; they were sharecroppers; the contracts they signed are in the William T. Johnson Collection.

Black Lake Plantation December 14, 1872

Dear Sister,

I write you a few lines to in form you that i am well and hope these few lines may find you and all the rest off the family well. Siss I want to tell you a bout that odd Barrell of Pork that Richard O Coner is a bout to Cheat you out off. The rations you sent for was hauled on the place monday, the forth day of march. The two wood choppers recived 4 pounds each witch made 8 pounds they left on the 9th of the month. They were the only wood choppers that got any rations out of that Barrell of pork. Now, i want to tell you what went with it. While jack work on the fence he gave him 12 pounds of meat he make jack pay it back. He traded 19 pounds pickle pork with green for 22 pounds of fresh meat. Dealia got tired eating pickel pork. He let alford witing have 28 pounds of meat. He got it back again an he let green have 4 pounds of meat for Bartlet, the time he fenced. So you see what went with the Barrell of pork. He fed it to Dealia and her Children. They finished fencing on the 26 day of april. So count now from the time the meat came to the time they quit fencing — 4th day of march to the 26th day of april. Now allow 4 pounds for Bartlet and 8 pounds [for] the wood chopers, 8 and 4 is 12. Is 12 pounds all the meat a barrell contains. Now sis, from 4th day of march to the 9th Day of march, could two men eat a barrel of pork or Could wilford eat a Barrel of pork weighting two hundred lbs from the 4 day of march to the 26 day of april, the time they quit fencing. I think not. Bob did not draw any meat out of the barrell. He used his own meat. From 4th day march to 26 day april is only 9 weeks and one day. Two short a time to eat two hundred pounds meat. Siss, look last year Books and where you see Deilia Page charged with 8 pounds of meat and two pecks of meal, 4 lbs of the meat i ishued to willford and one of the pecks of meal for him self and you will make him pay for it. Siss, be fore I finished my letter in looking through an old box i accidently came a cross the very book i had been looking for the last six month. I had given up all hopes of finding it when i picked up an old paper to read and out falls the very Book i had wanted, to prove Richard O' Coner the bigest liar that ever lived. Bob says Richard swore there was nothing on the Books Charged to wilford, so you see what a fare lie you have caught him in. Bob and tarry told me they herd page and Richard tell wilford when you asked him a bout the rations from last year to know nothing a bout it. Wilford came to the house and ask me if i had anything charged to him and i told him yes and he Could not say a word. So you se he is charged on my book with 44 lbs of meat and 11 pecks of meal. Meat was 15 cts a pound last year and meal 40 cts a peck so you may thank Bob for that much. He kept on telling me he saw me charge wilford with rations last year and made me hunt for the book untill i found it.[1]

Richard M. Johnson

1. Richard Conner, Delia Page and her children, Mr. Whiting, Alfred, Jack, Bob, and Bartlett sharecropped with Richard Johnson at Black Lake Plantation.

Ascension,[1] January 9th, 1876

Miss Anna,

Dear friend,

Your welcome letter of the 4th inst. came safely to hand finding me well and glad to hear from you. I also received by the same mail a letter from my sister in which she informed me of my Brother's marriage. I was considerably surprised as I had no Idea his mind was in that direction. Your letter now before me is nearer like those written when we first began our correspondence and I will try to answer as it deserves, but I thought Sometime back that I might be tiring you with answering so often letters which might not be interesting to you. I am glad to hear you enjoyed the holidays so well. No, I am not so busily engaged as you suppose, but will always have time to write to you. As I said before, we have pretty fair times here last Monday night. Myself, a friend & Mrs. La, & Sister went to a ball and fair given by the I'ville[2] firemen. We had a pretty nice time and stayed till 2 oclock in the morning. It was the first Public Affair I attended and I had an opportunity of seeing the French in all their glory. The only drawback was that I could not understand the general conversation. I would like to have that young lady tell my fortune, but not in Company; although, what she said about the letter might have been the same if you had received the letter from some other Gentlemen's friend. I wish we lived 2 miles apart instead of 200. Then probably we might make ourselves understood. I would like to hear that lecture you promised to give me the next time we sit on the same sofa, or I believe you wished me to be directly opposite to you. Do you still think you can read my thoughts or Judge by my countenance whether I am answering truly. This "missive" will be posted in New Orleans to morrow so I think you will receive it by next Thursday. You ought not to allow your Brother to take your letters from the Office if he keeps them so long in his pocket. Send Virginia and you will be sure to get them. On the 27th of this month, 24 years ago, I was in Natchez. Where I will be that many years later, I would like to know. Tomorrow will be sunday. Maybe I will go to Church, where I have not been since I left St Louis. That is not a good plan, is it? I dated this one day ahead because I am writing at night and it will soon be midnight. Why do you think I have more to do and think about now than before? My little Niece wrote a few lines to me to day in which she inquired for you. She is getting along well at School and writes a good letter for a girl of 11. I sometimes remind her of mistakes in her letters, but she answers by correcting mine, so I think in a few years more, she will have it all to herself, and I will have nothing more to say. I believe I told you about Mrs. Morgan's sister going to her house in Illinois. She went with the intention of staying, but after enjoying the Cold winds up there a few weeks she concluded to come back which she did a short time ago. The Planters here are busy planting a new crop and expect to raise ⅛ more sugar or Kane than last year which with last years crop I think will make times better for all. Miss Kate must have a lonesome time of it Teaching in the country and by herself.[3] Give my regards to all inquiring friends. I will look for an answer by the 18th of this month and as I have tried to reply in full to your last I shall hope for another just like it. With what addition you can think of. I wish you a happy New Year and hope that this, and many others to come will bear you on to peace, happiness, & prosperity. Good bye. For the present. From Yours truly.

T L Coleman

P.S. I wrote a letter to my sister in St. Louis the same time I wrote to you last and to day got an answer from her & one from you. So it seems a letter will go to St. Louis and back as quick as to Natchez & back. T. L. C.

1. Ascension Parish, Louisiana.

2. Iberville, Louisiana.

3. By 1876, Catharine Johnson was teaching in a country school near Ravenwood, Mississippi.

Ascension La., January 21st, 1876

Miss Anna: Dear friend,

Your welcome letter dated Jan 14th came to hand this morning finding me well and glad to hear from you. You say you can tell my letters at a glance. Well, if it were not for my Sister Joe's letters, I would recognize yours, but I have taken one of yours and one of hers and placed them side by side, and, if it were not for the Post Mark, could not tell whether it was from you or from her. Yes, you have often said you never tire of *hearing* from your friends, but I dont remember your saying anything about not tiring of *writing* to them. I have not heard the particulars of the marriage and dont remember of even seeing the Lady. Her name was Boid. How I shall like my Sister in law I will tell you by & by. As I suppose I will see her sometime, sooner or later. Yes, I think you might be present if that young lady told my fortune, for I've just got conceit enough about me to think that she could not prejudice you against me even if her predictions were not of the flowery kind. Of course, you will say she could but then you know I will risk it. You have no other Gentlemen correspondents. Well, I had completely forgotten that but I will say that I have but one Lady Correspondent, outside of my family. Now judging by what you said about present company, you wont believe that. Again, you may say yes because those that I would otherwise write to are near enough to see. Yes, but still I do not see them. There will be a marriage here about the 15th of March and I will write you, all about it. Yess, I meant that wish and would decrease the space, regardless of the increase of miles from this part & that is more than I can expect you to agree to. No I have never amused myself either before or since in anyone's company as much as in yours. What you said about thoughts not directed up stream but floating down. It is all very well to talk about, but you know better than that. I have not seen or heard from Mr Morgan or his family since the time I wrote you about it. I know nothing of Miss Morgan's feeling with regard to the climate or Company of either of her homes. I will not undertake to say why she came back. I think you would enjoy Mrs. M's company if you were acquainted with her. She is about as inteligent & witty a little lady, for she is small, as I have met with for some time. Give my regards to your Sisters. I would like to receive a Natchez paper once in a while. To day, the Williamson Co. murderer — Crain Marshall — will be hung or hanged. I suppose you have heard or read of him. The weather here is remarkably fine and Planters taking advantage of it to plant their Cane. I hope to receive an answer from you — and a long one too — by the 3rd of February next. At this rate our letters will not be like "Angels Visits." Maybe all those remarks or accusations were applicable to yourself. And that *your* thoughts instead of floating "placidly" down the way were quietly anchored somewhere in the neighborhood of Natchez and that writing to me was merely to kill dull time or for want of something to amuse you. And that some time not far distant I would hear you had quietly floated from this single state of Existence in to the double rule of two and left me to consider, at my liesure, the ways of woman. When this "missive" reaches you remember I am down in Cajindom awaiting your reply. Good bye for the present hoping to hear from you soon I remain as ever.

Yours Truly
T. L. Coleman

Feb 24th, 1876
Ascension Parish.
Allimania Post Office

Miss Anna,

I received your welcome letter to day and was glad to hear from you. I felt sure all this time your long looked for letter was lost and now I know it. I told you in my last not to direct to I'ville anymore as I am certain it is there my letters are lost. So you will be careful in future not to put the old directions on again. I am sorry your letter did not reach me for I hate to have my letters, or those sent to me, fall in to other hands, than those they were intended for. Maybe the letter never left Natchez. The Mardi Gras seems to be the order of the day here. Mrs. L. and Sister goes to New Orleans next Monday to see it. As for myself, I must say my experience in last Mardi Gras will satisfy me for some time yet. No, I have neither sent, nor received my valentines this year, nor for some time back. I think I will have to close this letter as I did one some time ago by saying I had a good deal to say but could not think of it. I have not received a line from my Brother since he was married, So to day I wrote to him for some Building plans, and after writing a few lines on common place matters I closed the letter and added a P.S. telling him to give my regards to Mrs. D.C. She has never seen me, so I suppose she will think I am a perfect Bear. We had considerable rain here for the last week, and plenty of wind; so that we have to stay in the House pretty close. I have formed a new acquaintence since I wrote or rather acquaintences for there's a family. Very nice people too but unfortunately they are living twelve miles from here. Still we — Myself & a relation of theirs manage to ride them in 1½ hours. And you know from that we are not the slowest riders in the world. I promised to go up there Mardi Gras day, but the Lady portion of our household are going to the City so there will be only Mr L and myself at home. My trip will have to go by the board. I hope you will write a good long letter next time and that you will feel more like writing than I do to night. I will close with regards to all. Goodbye for the present.

Yours Truly
T. L. Coleman

Direct to *Allimania*, La. Post Office

 ───────────────────────────

Ravenwood, December 8, 1877

Dear Sister,

Your ever welcome letter came safely to hand after a long week of anxious waiting. I am happy to hear that all of you are well, but sorry to hear that Mr. Carlito's cough has returned. I am afraid unless he is more careful that cough will result in something serious. I am glad that you got my check cashed in time to assist you a little with your taxes for they have been a heavy burden on my mind. I could hardly realize the fact that poor unfortunate I had received the reward for one month labor at last.

I did not think that Robinson & Jim Johnson would make much but had no idea that their crop would fall so short as that — but they have done Just what I suspected — stolen the crop our of the field & as they have dealt with us so I hope the Lord will deal with them.

What has become of Richard? You never mention him. As for your intended visitors, all that I can say is "Lord Forbid." It seems that we are put into this world to hear the burdens of others even though we are sinking under our own. But I think under the circumstances you would be justifiable in down right refusing to bear this burden. As I am afraid that it will prove the "straw that will break the Camel's back." I am sorry to hear of Ockie's[1] misfortune. Poor little Ockie! Her lot is like ours — full of misfortunes & trials of all kinds.

We have been having dreadful weather here up to today & yesterday, when it ceased raining & turned quite cold. But the people are out to day picking as hard as they can. To day is the first time that I have gone to the school house since it has been raining so I have taught at home. They have fixed the stove in the school house at last & are now holding a protracted meeting. I have not been yet but expect to go one night this week.

Cy Darcy has been here every Sunday since I arrived here to see if I was going to Church. I put him off with every excuse about the weather that I could think of. So this Sunday he came and offered to get a buggy and horse which quite exhausted my patience so I told him when I felt like going to Church I could find the way there by myself. Then he remarked perhaps his company was not acceptable to which I made no reply & so I have not seen the Gent since.

Tell Alice that I will try and get some potatoes & eggs to bring home, So far, pecans, they are kind hard to get ahold of. Eggs are 23 cents a dozen. Butter the same, 23 cents. Geese are $3 three Dollars a piece. You have not told me whether you have swapted off Betsey[2] or not. Mr. Wallace wanted me to bring her up here and he would take care of her, but I thought that it would be too much trouble.

I have only taken in enough money to pay two dollars and six bits of my board. More owed me. I hear Mrs Wallace's lessons sometimes and she wanted to deduct a dollar from my board but I think that three Dollars is little enough to cook — wash for a person for. Don't you?

Kiss poor little Ockie for me & write as often as you can for when I dont hear from home I cant sleep. Give my love to Jo & Alice, Mrs. Sterns,[3] Julia, Mary's Julia & all enquiring friends & you except the same from you affectionate Sister

Kate

1. Oakie Sterns, the daughter of Catharine Lynch Johnston and Clarence Johnston (Johnson).
2. The family's cow.

3. Mrs. Sterns was a friend of the Johnsons. She and her husband had been free people of color before the war. Her husband, Washington Sterns, had been a friend and business associate of William T. Johnson.

Ravenwood, February 8th, 1878

Dear Sister

I write you a few lines to let you know that I am still in the land of the living. I would have written before, but came off from home without any ink & the store on the place being closed, I could get none until today when I succeeded in getting a little bit of a bottle of this blue stuff for a Nickle.

I had quite a pleasant trip up on the boat. Em's prediction came true in this particular. I did meet a fair man on the boat — who was no less a personage than Mr Henry Smith. He was quite attentive, presented me with a bundle containing some apples oranges & bananas. He inquired for Mrs Sterns' Ockie, & Jo. He said that he was just from Natchez, but had no time to call while there.

I arrived at L'Argent about three O'Clock & was just leaving the boat with Mr Shumaker, when Mr Dent come running up the Stairs. I did not recognize him at first, but he came up and spoke. I took his arm then & Mr Shumaker went to see about my trunk.

Mr Dent was very kind, he escorted me to my room after we reached Mr Porter's, kindled a nice fire in the stove & we sat down for a little chat. I told him all the News that I could think of, not omitting the kiss that Mr Barland give you and Ockie. When I was ready to retire he pulled of [f] his overCoat & added it to my bed clothing which was rather thin. In the Morning I had quite a nice breakfast of fried chicken eggs, fish, coffee, biscuits, & butter. I waited untill after nine OClock & No one came for me so Mr. D. sent me over in a buggy at his expense, he was very kind indeed.

They were not expecting me for Mr. Wallace had left the Place & had not received my letter. He and his wife separated for good this time & he has Moved off the place. I am staying at Mrs Bowman's.

I have Enrolled 20 pupils up to the present date. Anna, I want you to see if Mr Donaldson would let me have some books. I want Eight second Readers — McGuffy's two third Readers. Eight — Robinson's Primary Arithmatic & three Rudiments, two 1st readers. One Man has given me a dollar to get his little girl some books. But I want you to send all that I send for right of & those who do not pay for them. I will Not let them have them. Please send them up as soon as possible. Give my love to

Mrs. S., Alice, Ockie, Josie, Catharine & kiss the baby for me. I Miss her so much.

I left my umbarel either at Mr. Porter's or on the boat coming from School Yesterday. I was caught in the rain I suppose that is what set my tooth to aching. I have no fire in my School room either, so it matters not how cold it gets. I will have to stand it. I suppose that it is useless to complain to the Board. Be sure to send the books. Again with love to all & to yourself. I remain.

Your Affectionate Sister

Kate Johnston

P.S. Give my love to Mrs Delia, Mrs Betsey, the Children, Julia, & the Children.

K Johnston [1]

Tell Ockie that I will write to her when I get more settled.

1. By the 1870s the Johnson siblings had begun to change the spelling of their name to "Johnston," as Catharine did in this letter. A considerable number of freed slaves had taken the name Johnson after the war, and the Johnson siblings would have wanted to retain their unique identities by separating themselves from freed people.

·Ravenwood March 12

Dear Sister

Your welcome letter came safely to hand finding me well. I am glad to hear that all are well at home. I guess Johnny's sickness is nothing more serious than an overwhelming desire to remain in Town a few days.

I am glad to see that the Natchez Ladies are having a little pleasure this year & are not all like us, chained to the Rock of adversity — bound there by masculine mismanagement & indolence, not a little mixed with meanness.

I am sorry to hear of the Stock diminishing so. I am afraid that Place was a bad investment.

Yes, I heard about them trying to move my School. I guess they will succeed after a while. I sent you a letter Saturday containing $3.00. I still owe you now forty-five cents. I will send you ten cents in this letter & ten cents in Ockie's letter. I sent you my Report I suppose that you received it & hope that when you go to collect it that they will pay that $40.00 also.

Sunday before last, mr Shumaker was over to see me. I dont think that he looks well. He says that he had some difficulty in getting a place to teach at first that the people did not want to allow the use of the Church for School purposes unless the School Board would allow the $20.00 per Month, but he at last convinced them that they would never be able to get sent from the Board, so they consented to let him have the use of it.

Mrs. Beauman's daughter Colleen came home to her father last week with two dreadful cuts in her head where her husband struck her with a large stick. She started to the Magistrates, but stopped at her father's until morning. The next Morning, she said that her head pained her so that she could not go. Her Mother and father were both much troubled, her Mother dressed her wounds & told her to rest easy that she would take her husband to court. Colleen sit around the house all the morning but in the evening they missed her, her Mother, thinking that she had gone to some of the neighbors sent her little brother when it grew dark after her with a shawl, but Colleen had gone home even so far, through the woods, & with that broken head — walked back to her husband. Her Mother was rampant. I could not help from laughing. She said I tell you what Miss Johnston I would not go to see her again if she was dying I would not have gone before but it looked so bucus. I had to go, I told her she ought not to talk on for that bucus feeling would compel her to go again if anything happened to Colleen.

I lost my little red bow going to School this morning — I miss it so much. I left my old black alpaca skirt home and I can hardly get along without it.

Give my love to all both relatives and friends and accept the same from

Your Affectionate Sister
K.G. Johnston [1]

1. Catharine Geraldine Johnson; "K." is short for "Kate," her nickname.

Troyville La. February 23rd, 1888

Miss K.G. Johnston,

Dear Miss,

Your letter of the Feb 21st inst. [came] to hand this morning and I will hasten to answer. Yes, we need a Teacher for this place. And if you will come right away, we will be glad to have you. We have been promised by so many, and they have disappointed us every time. We hardly know whether to look for one now, or not when they say they want to come Our public School will last three months. And for the first class examination $40.00. Second Class $80.00 and board. I will charge just whatever you are willing to pay.

Now if you will come right on, we will be glad to have you do so as we are tired of being disappointed. I will look for you this week sure.

Hope that you will come right on.

I am Respectfully
Lizzie Hayes
Troyville, La.

 _____

Natchez March the 9th, 1888

Miss Anna
Dear Sister,

Anna, I write you these few lines to find out why you do not write. I have been so anxious to hear whether you saw the Superintendent and what he had to say. And Josephine asked me to send out word to her if I heard from you and each day this week the Mail has arrived, with no letter from you. I hope you met with success, and are not sick. Even if you are, you should have let us hear from you.

I am not feeling at all well Myself. I have a soreness in my side. Pauline rubbed it for me last night, but it is there still.

Billy went over for Annie on last Sunday, but has not arrived with her yet. I think they look for him about Sat. Josephine and Johnny's school will close today, but I do not know when to look for Alice as she lost so much time in this Month. She has not been in since you left, but Harriet has. Johnny's[1] mouth is healing up very rapidly. He was saying his prayers the other night to Josephine and when she came to the end of the prayer, Johnny said to her, "Aunt Joe you have not said all yet." "She asked him what she had left out," and he told her to ask me what it was So he stayed on his knees and I heard his prayer and made him pray for you. That was the part She had left out.

They are giving a series of little entertainments for the purpose of raising class money. Mrs. Winston had one at her house last night, but feeling badly I did not go. Chum has one to night. Our Institute meets to morrow, but if I am not feeling better I dont think I shall attend that either, though I should like to do so. Pauline and Steve are well and send love to you. Pauline has been real anxious about you. All the children keep well. I believe Man is looking for Catharine home tomorrow. I for one will be glad though I doubt whether I will be any more relieved from the worry with the children. I have not seen Mr. D. since you left. That is, he has not been to the house. I got Jane to help Josephine to iron Sat. and afterward she scrubbed your room and wiped out the wall, and I the gallery and the steps. I have sent Ellen and Jane up and had Agnes and Emerline brought down. Betsey is dead & so is one of Josephine's cows. They got bogged and was so weak before they got them out. They did not recover from it. Mrs. K. and everyone over there send love to you. And the same from home. Mrs. Sterns is here still. I suppose she went out, and countermanded her first order. I remain your affectionate sister.

Miss Anna L. Johnston

I sent you five Dollars. Did you receive it?

1. Probably the son of William Johnson Jr.

Troyville, March 13th, 1888

Dear Sister

I received your letter and was very sorry that my silence caused you uneasiness: but the truth of it is, it has been so cold that I could not write in my room on account of having no fire, and rather than write in Mrs Hayes's room I thought that I would wait untill the weather became more pleasant.

I am quite troubled about that pain in your side. I think that you ought to consult Dr. Metcalf and not wait until it culminates in a sick spell. I guess that it is worry and cold that is the matter with you more than anything else. My life here is so quiet and peacable that I can scarcely realize that it is my self.

I was quite provoked to hear of that accident to Johnnie's face. Kiss the little fellow and tell him that I want to see the two little Johnnies so badly.

What can be the matter with Mr. D. I guess the old Lady has frightened him off.

Troyville is a quiet little town, but seems to be growing very fast. It is high too, and they tell me it takes quite an overflow to submerge it. They are talking of a rail-road passing through — it — which I think should render property here more valuable.

The house that I am in at present could be bought for six hundred Dollars, and it has quite a large yard. True, the house needs much repairing, but then the lot is worth more than that.

I was surprised when at Harrisonburg to see the number of colored people who owned their own little homes. So many of the men are working at what they call the sack work for which they receive one Dollar and a half per day.

I could not see much of the town for it rained the whole time that I was up there.

They have but very poor accomodations for a school so far as school furniture is concerned. I have for my desk a large box with the sides knocked out. For benches, I have three long planks nailed onto some blocks, which sometimes in the midel of a recitation, will give way and let the children down on the floor in a heap. I have enrolled but twenty-one up to date and find them very obedient but not at all advanced in their studies. The highest being in the third reader.[1]

What has become of Mr. L. You never mention him. Remember me to him when you see him.

Tell Josephine that I feel for her that she has to bear the burden alone, but three months will soon roll away. How is Gena getting along. Who is going to teach in Catharine's place? Give my love to Man, though I don't suppose that he ever thinks of me. Did you receive the letter that I wrote you last week? send me a newspaper now and then, I have nothing in the world to read. Give my love to all at home and all over to Mrs. Delia's

Write soon.

> Your Affectionate Sister
> Kate G. Johnston

1. This letter, and those preceding it, point up the difficult conditions under which the women taught.

> Troyville Mar 23rd, 1888

Dear Sister,

I received your ever welcome letter with great pleasure for it has been sometime since I have heard from home. I had begun to think that something had happened. I dreamed. I dream of home so much.

I received the basket with contents all safe except the clock. That I found to be perfectly useless so far as keeping time is concerned. It ticks on faithfully, but the hands remain stationary. I was quite disappointed about it so I take in and dismiss by guess.

I have enrolled 28 pupils up to date and have but two as far advanced as the third reader.

I thought I told you that I have a contract for $40.00. Now if they do not find some excuse for not giving it to me.[1]

Mr. Block came to see me yesterday and seemed very glad when I told him that I had secured a public school. He asked me how I was getting along; if I had been well, and how I passed my time. He seemed pleased when I told him they had had no dances since I had been here. Said he was glad to hear it for he had feared something of the kind. He told me if I needed money, or anything else just to let him know, and he wishes that I would try and get the Vidalia School again. He does not like Mrs Miller at all.

There was peddler boarding here a few weeks ago by the name of Mr. Louis. He left for Natchez Sunday a week ago. He was quite anxious for me to send you a letter by him. I told him I had just written so he said he would find you and take my compliments and told me if I wanted to go home he would pay my way. I thanked him, but told him I did not want to go. He kept on insisting on me going until I asked him what was the matter with him. He knew that I was teaching. Well, he said "take good care of yourself. I dont see how you can stay busied here."

He brought me a package of candy before he left.

While I was in the Harrisonburg a colored or rather a black man there who spoke of moving to Mississippi. I told him of our Place and he said that he would go to Natchez soon and see you. He and his wife were very kind to me when I was in Harrisonburg. I am glad to hear that you are better. I knew some one needed the Dr. I saw him at our house as plainly. Give my love to Annie. I wish that I could see her before the home troubles makes her thin. Tell Jo she must write to me sometimes.

How are things getting along. You never mention the children, the boarders. I mean, did Julia ever come back?

And what are they doing on the Place? How is Eugenia getting along now? I think of home so much.

K.

1. The women were often paid in script, which was not always redeemed.

 _____

Natchez May 7, 1888

Dear Sister[1]

I received your much welcome letter with much pleasure and was happy to hear that you continued to have good health. I sent you your inching today I waited thinking that I would send altogether but it was so long before I could get into your trunk. I told Johnny to open it but he failed to do so, and got off before I asked whether he had done so or not. I sent to try and borrow a key but could not get one. I looked where you told me, but the key was not there. So as Johnny does not come from the Place until Sat. night I had to wait untill he came. And when he did come I gets him to go up stairs and open what I thought was your trunk but which proved to be Josephine's who like to have taken a fit about it. So I shall make another effort to open yours this time. This evening while I sewed Sacques and dress Josephine came from the Place[2] feeling right poorly, but is much better today.

How many more weeks have you to stay in Troyville? It seems like you have been gone such a long time.

Henry Dixon has been down with the Consumption a long while. Poor Miss Medora Ross died on Friday morning. She was perfectly resigned to her death.

The Russell family got into a terrible fracas with Charles Russell's lady love last week, but I would rather tell you about it when I see you.

We have had some very rainy weather for several days but it was much needed in the country. I have my cisterns finished at last I have only to let it dry, put a top on it, and a Pump or bucket, which ever I wish, when it will be all ready for water then for the gutters. Our examination comes off next Sat. and then that part of the trouble will be over. We will not have a School Exhibition this year, but will close with a Pic Nic of which I am very glad indeed. They have a right nice garden started at the Place. Mr. D. was down last night and seemed in a very good humor indeed. Mrs. Delia had not been well at all. She was at the house last evening and looked right weak. Pauline is some what ailing also. Laura Davis has moved and we are about to have other. . . .

I am real sorry as it cuts us off from our short way of visiting Mrs. D. Annie & Rosa are well and all send love. I get Ella to come every week to help iron so that Jo and Alice can leave on Tuesdays. There is to be a grand Concert here this week by Gilmore's famous Band. The price of admission is $2.00 and they sold five hundred tickets in an hour and a half. The Hall will not be large enough to accommodate the crowd that wishes to go. I am just as sleepy and stupid as I can be this evening. Alice, Jo, and everybody at home and over to Mrs. D.'s send love to you. Hoping to hear from you soon.

I remain

> Your Affectionate Sister,
> Anna L. Johnston

1. Catharine Johnson.

2. The Peachland Plantation purchased by the women.

Natchez February 28th 1889

Dear Sister

I write to you these few lines to inform you that I received your most welcome letter and was glad to hear from you. I would have answered sooner, but I have been so busy that I could not find time to write. Alice came in Thurs. evening and stayed until Sunday Evening. Harriet sends love to you, and requested me to tell you that Jimmie Conference Chavours had made his appearance at last. Yes, she has a little boy at last and I know she is proud.

Poor Mrs. Thompson died on Sat. morning and was buried Sunday Evening. The Firemen had had a grand parade on Fri and the day was lovely. They passed our house twice which I considered quite an honor, the more especially as they so frequently fail to pass here once.

Judge Reber is at the head of the street Railway Company again. His family are living on Union St.

Josephine is better than she was, though she still has a very bad cold. Sonny gets married tomorrow night. I suppose I will have to go, if the weather is favorable. Pauline will go also. I don't know whether Josephine will go or not yet. Josie came in on Sat. and stayed until Sunday morning.

Anna Hargrave was up too. She came up on Fri. night and went down this morning. Alice, Pauline, and myself went to a Masque Party on Friday night at Mrs. [illegible text]. Alice did not mask, but Pauline and myself did. We masked quite successfully too. Evangeline said I looked nice and some how, it looked to her that fine clothes belonged to me. I send some more papers with this letter. I am glad they afford you pleasure.

Three of the cows at the Place have calves. I sent Pat notice to leave on Sat. I did not do so before because he said he was going of his own accord. I sent Man up to the Place last week and he planted some Irish Potatoes, and broke up near about three Acres of land in pat's field that used to be. He used Prince, and Ebb and this week Bush will plow the oxen. I am going to try & make something someway. . . .[1]

1. The final page of this letter is missing. The handwriting is that of Anna, and it appears that she wrote the letter to Catharine.

Natchez, Mar. 31st 1895

Dear Sister,

I thought I would drop you a few lines to relieve your mind of any anxiety you might feel respecting the examination.

We have decided to take the third one instead of the first. Mr. Ker says he thinks it will be best of us to wait, so that he can find out whether there will be any change in the nature of the Examinations or not. He was under the impression that having made a State Certificate of 1st Grade & having taught under it 5 yrs that he was exempt from examination anymore. But under the new State-law he, Miss Mary, & I suppose Mr. Henderson will have to undergo another one. Miss Irving was tellimg me about it Fri. She says there must be something rotten in Denmark.

Nevis did not get out until Wed. past. The day she came down to go the week before, Josie was so sick, that it looked as if it would break her heart to leave her. She tried to control her feelings but could not, so she cried & said that she could not leave Aunt Jo. So Josie told me that when she saw Nevis enter the door, it was like an angel entering it. I dont know what will become of her, she gets a little better and then goes back as bad as ever. Duck has been sick for two or three days, but is better now & up again.

Pauline came home Fri. and complained of her right eye feeling as if it had grit in it, but she sat up late Fri. night and wrote down things for Examinations use & the consequence was, she suffered all night & though it is much better still she has to sit in her rocker with a bandage on it. She hopes to be able to go to school to morrow.

I went up to the Place on last Fri. Evening. Eddie B. took me up. I had to come home early Sat. to get the things needed as I met the wagon coming in, as I was going out. Holiday had things moving lively. He came down Fri. night, but is going right back this Evening. He has planted already about 20 acres of corn & some potatoes and is going to plant more & All of Dudley's field, except the extreme lower end is plowed up. He is going to put peas in that part that D. did not break up last year. He is going to have a little Blacksmith Shop on the Place.

Alice & harriet came in yesterday morning & went out in the Evening. It rained steady all day. I went to see Rosa Foster, and found a wreck of her former self. She seemed very glad to see me, she said it seemed to her that I rested on her mind & she had to see me. She sent work to me by two or three. Mabel has been keeping very close or rather her Mother has kept her so. I was out there the other Evening and she was so glad to see me. All the family join me in sending love to you and Annie. I received a letter from A.K. the other day; all of them send love. She says they have a fine garden. Study all you can. I will send for you in time.

Your Affectionate Sister

Anna

March 1899

Dear Sister,

You can never understand how bitterly I am disappointed when I fail to get home at the end of the month. I look forward to my visit with such longing as only one like myself — having a home yet never being allowed to enjoy it — can feel. Then I think the change would be beneficial, this sameness is telling on my health and spirits.

I arose early Saturday morning and prepared to go to town as Mary Ellen had promised to take me. But it began to rain and when the mule came that she had borrowed to take me in with he was so fractious she was afraid to drive him and I was afraid to ride behind him. For it matters not how things are. I do not wish my life to end wiolently.

Mary Ellen speaks of going in tomorrow, but I do not wish to lose another day, and will let her go alone. Pay her for me and send me some soap. I am much obliged for the paper and envelopes and would have written before, but had but one stamp and fearing that disappointment might again crown my hopes of getting home. I kept it to send my report by mail.

I shall send this letter by mail for fear that Mary E. might not get off to-morrow.

Anna, I wish that you would lend me a white apron. Mine is nearly worn out, and I must have something to conceal the spots on my dress. I hate to bother you, but you know a body's wants will cry out sometimes, however hard one may strive to stifle them.

I have a little pig that was made a present to me and will try to get Mary Ellen to take him in for me if he does not get away again. Tell Jo to take care of it for me. Its mother is such a fine sow. Get Jim to put up a little pen for it. Tell Alice I feel a little jealous when I hear of her being in as often while I get in so seldom. There are many little things that I need but refrain from mentioning because I feel that I am a broken spoke in the wheel this year as all that I earn must go to the Dr.

God only knowns what another year may bring forth. I trust better things.

Tell Jo I received my books and they were quite a pleasure to me. I found some of them very interesting. I should have another Hearth and Home by this time.

My eyes pain me so that I can not read much at night. That little present that I spoke of if you could get me some little cheap presents in glass ware like tumblers or something of that kind that is useful, I would be very glad.

I have a good enrollment this month, but that cold spell reduced my average. I suppose not having an assistant will work against me for the people want their children early now and you know it is impossible to do justice to them and let them out early. But it is a still greater injustice to reduce my salary for asking for me when the school needs it. Hoping to hear from you soon for I do not know when I shall see you all. I remain your affectionate sister.

K.G. Johnston

Love to all at home
The weather is getting pleasant. You might send for me some Friday.

The Diary *of*

Catharine Geraldine Johnson,

1864–1874

Tuesday Natchez May the 10, 1864

It has been a gloomy day for May. The rain has been falling all day. It has been hailing also. And to night the wind is wild and whistling through the tree grove more like dreary autumn than bright sunny May. Hark, how the rain falls sadly on the housetop and the wind howls. Oh, how mournfully. . . . To me it sounds like the Cries of sorrow. Yet I love the sound for at present it becomes well my feelings which are like the day, gloomy and sad.

Day is gone and still and silent night is here, the time for calm reflection. Silence reigns over the whole house. All are asleep but me. I am restless and wakefull. My mind goes back to the past with its Joys and sorrows. Back to the time when we were *happy thoughtless children* when the earth seemed to be one abode of happiness I grieve to think how quickly the scene changed. Our home was so happy until. . . . No, I will not write of that dark time. Suffice it to say it fills my soul with a bitterness that will remain for-ever. I cannot *forget* & I cannot *forgive*. . . . I have done nothing but sew a little to day. And no one has been to the house. I don't care much for company now. Annie received a long letter from W G[1] to day. How hope-full and affectionate he writes.

1. William Gardner.

Sunday May the 22 1864

I have not written any since Tuesday the 10. How lazy. I shall never make a good Chronicleir. Well, I can only write when I feel like it which is not often. My heart is aching so much that I can barely think and Mr. Gardner came down on Thursday. He had only been gone a week and his return was quite unexpected though none the less welcome. I was so glad to see him again. Though we kept him waiting some time before we went in to the parlor. That could not be helped. We had to make our toilet (being in our dishabiller). Making ones toilet takes quite a time. After we had finished dressing ourselves we went in to the parlor and he had just gone up the street. When he returned we were waiting in the parlor. He came running in, his face all aglow with the pleasure of seeing us. He did not come for-ward to meet us. But stood for a while and looked at us. Then exclaiming

Well I am here again. Which one of you shall I take first. He came forward shook hands with Anna first and Kissed her. Then shook hands and kissed the rest of us. He seemed so happy. One could easily see that His pleasure was infaigne. But it is not strange that he should be happy here for he loves Anna Deeply. That I can see. I thought so at first, but now I know my first impressions were correct. I do not know wether she loves him in return. I can not tell. She is a strange girl and so reserved.

Thursday the 26 [May] 1864

It is very cloudy to day. I think it likely that we will have some rain before night. I should be glad of it as it is very dusty. Nothing of importance has transpired during the week. Everything goes on in the same hum drum stile. Only William seems to grow worse. I am afraid he will lose his mind entirely. He sets talking to himself and laughing in a manner that is very annoying to us particularly when strangers are here. I wish that he could be once more like he was before his marriage and the miserable time that succeeded it. Alas, I fear that happiness for him is over. He is a perfect wreck of his former self.[1] So much for not heeding the advice of his family and friends. Anna received a letter from Mr Gardner Friday. He is in Tennessee on his way to join the regiment.[2] He dont expect to return until the Campaing is ended which I think might last all summer. She says he had three narrow escapes from Death. He seems to have so much faith in Gods Protecting power. His heart must be pure or else he could not write like that. he is so true and firm in his affections how may they alwas continue as stedfast. He calls Anna his darling and me his sister. He seems to love her so I wonder if she has given him any encouragement. He looks it or rather acts like it. I would ask her, but I know that she would just look at me and with a quiet smile just tell me I had too much curiosity. Ah well I suppos iff she wont tell me I never find out. I hope he may come back safe and unchanged. Mr. Wieker was up to see us to day, only stayed two or three hours. He say Paulin[3] and friends are coming up. I hope she may for I do so long to see her.

1. William, Catharine's oldest brother, had mental problems for many years. He was eventually declared insane and hospitalized in New Orleans.
2. William Gardner joined the Fifth Regiment of the Confederate Army.
3. Pauline; Catharine spells the name two ways.

August the 2, 1865[1]

This is the commencement of another month. Again I take my pencil to write a few lines in my neglected diary. Old friend, I seldom come to thee except in moments of unhappy thought and feeling when such thoughts as I can not express to a human being like myself. Strange to say I never express a serious thought to anyone. How can I blame people then if they look upon me as light and frivolous, incapable of understanding or entertaining serious thoughts. They cannot think otherwise when I only show one side of my character to them. O, if I could only get over the strange affliction that seals my life upon each serious subject, but I suppose it is useless to wish for. I fear that my nature is constitutionally defective. I am morally a coward. I lack the free independance so necessary to a happy exsistance. No my will is too meak. I am too ready to listen to others in oppinion when I should be firm and unyielding.

1. This entry is incorrectly dated. The date should read "August the 2, 1864." This entry was recorded between May and August 1864, and the diary was kept in a bound volume.

August Tuesday the 16 1864

To day have received papers stating that another large Battle has been fought, in which the 5 s had been literally cut to pieces. God grant that the life of one who has become dear to us may be spared. Just two short months and 17 day since he was with us full of life and hope. Now he is far away engaged in a cruel and bloody strugle the issue of which no mortal can tell.[1] To night who knows but that he may be among the fated ones that fell. Eleven days ago — I can not bear to think it so. Alas when we part from our friends And breath the simple word goodby how little know we what may transpire ere we feel the friendly clasp of their hand again. Sometimes when we part as we are thinking only for a few weeks long Dreary months and years intervene ere we meet again. And sometimes the dark word forever is written above that parting scene. But that such may not be present case I can only hope.

1. Catharine is speaking of William Gardner in this passage.

Aug Saturday the 20, 1864   going to rain

To day is gloomy and dull. It has been raining all day long. I wish it would stop. It makes me feel so bad. It looks as though it is going to rain all day. I feel strangely to day. I can't even think calmly. O, I am so tired of this constant quarreling unhappy life. I would give anything for the quiet home we once possessed. Now everything has changed. Richard and William just destroys the peace of the whole house. They are mean and seem devoid of all principle.

Friday August 25

I had promised my self that I would never give way to such bursts of passions. Oh, but alas I have this day broken that promise and spoken bitter wicked words. I cannot help it. Mine is an undisciplined nature. I do not understand myself. How can I expect to be understood by others.

Sept the 16th, 1864

I received a letter from Paulin this morning, but some how after waiting so long it did not satisfy me. It was not so interesting as some of her letters. Perhaps she did not feel in a writing mood, but when I get a letter and they do not answer to my expectations it makes me sad and gloomy. I feel in a complaining mood to day anyway. It seems that our troubles will never end. If I feel happy in the morning, something is sure to transpire be fore night to fret and anger me. Yesterday Leila was here and Rose also.[1] And we had quite a pleasant little time. After they left, we was all setting in the Gally, laughing and talking, when Jim came up with the news that Clifton had gone off with some recruiting Officer.[2] We was in hopes that he would never leave us, but turned out like everything, to be all hopes. I suppose it is no use grieving after spilt milk. I have not said any thing else to William about the horse thing, though he still continues to use her. (Contrary to his promise). Ma says she thinks that I had better let him have her for a while. I guess that I had better follow the advice, as she haves advised me wrong though it is against my inclination to favor William on account of his unjust and overbearing disposition. I must stop writing now and go to my sewing.

1. Free women of color who lived outside of Natchez.
2. Jim and Clifton were slaves belonging to the Johnsons.

[Undated entry][1]

I answered Pauline's letter to day, heard Josephine recite her lessons, practiced my music lesson. That has been the Amount of my days work so I can just count to day lost. Johanah was over here last night and she was telling us of her Aunts wicked treatment of her. She spoke so sadly of her condition and that of her little brother. Poor girl, I felt so sorry for her. She has suffered so much. I did not think that her wild nature was so capable of such deep feeling.

1. This entry is undated but because it appears between September 16 and October 25, it would have been written in late September or early October 1864.

October the 25, 1864

I arose rather late this morning — in fact, every morning this week. Consequently I have been behind in my duties.

Monday Oct. the 31 1864

The last night of the second fall month — how fast time flies. And how unimproved by me. I thought to accomplish so much ere the winter set in, but so far have accomplished nothing. Mason[1] returned this morning after an absence of four or five months. I was setting at the window in my room sewing when I saw him coming up the street. I watched him approach with a feeling of calm indifference mixed with a little arrogance for now thought I, I am to be bothered with him again. He seems unchanged in his feeling toward me and but for my coldness would have brought up the same old subject. Perhaps I am cruelly cold, but what is the use. I dont love. And hope that I never shall. And if I relax any he will take it for encouragement.

I wrote to Paulin on saturday. So did Anna. I expected a letter from her thursday. I must have been correct about my suspicion about that letter.

Now I think the manner in which I returned it made them angry from there subsequent action. It is pretty evident they expected something different. I am sleepy and must stop writing for the night.

1. James Mason, a free man of color and a resident of Adams County, Mississippi.

Nov. 1, 1864

It is late and Ma says that I must go to bed and not be burning out the light, but I will [write] a few lines before I retire. It has been raining all day to, but in spite of the inclemency of the weather Ja Mason came around to the house. I was determined not to have a private tate a tate with him to day so I managed to have him come in Ma's room instead of the parlor so that all the family would be in there. He asked for some music, but I did not feel in a mood for singing so I took my guitar and played a few pieces, but that did not satisfy him. He wanted me to sing. And I was glad when Ma began a conversation which was kept up until it was time for him to go or rather return for he is spending the night with Richard. Johanah was over this evening too with her usual kind of witt and hummour. How full of mischief the girl is. Poor Anna, she has the tooth ache all day. In fact, for two or three days. She is looking quite bad from it. Oh, I hope she will be rid of it by tomorrow.

Nov. the 3 Thursday [1864]

I did not write any last night being to tired and sleeppy, but the day passed without any event of significance taking place. The day being a bad one no one came to the house, but Mason. Toward night Wade came bringing the paper home we had loaned to Ceila and her sister. Also a note from Ceila to Anna excusing her long absence. It was not written in her usual hand which I know was done to avert suspicion from her as being the author of that letter. Bet she did not obtain her object. Any suspicions point just the same way. Yesterday was unpleasant very, but it was made so by the gloomy weather. And not by any wrong act of Anna, as to day was.

At the close of yesterday, I had nothing to reproach my self with as I have to night. It happened thus. I had finished writing and set down to sew.

Alice,[1] being seated near me. I reached over and took a spool of thread out of her lap when she attempted to prevent and said the thread was to fine for the garment that I was making. I insisted on having it and at last succeeding getting it. Then she said when she got it back that I should have no more of it. A spirit of Contrariness took possession of me then and I made an attempt to put it in my jacket, but she stayed my hand. Then I took her sewing and she, of course, snatched mine. And we both ran into the passag. And I got angry then. And we had quite an earnest little struggle and after the struggle I took her work and threw it down stairs. And when she asked for the thread I threw it behind the bed. I also spoke bitterly to her which I know hurt her feelings for all of which my conscious heavily concerns me, for I was in the wrong. How I am truely sorry that I acted that way. How I pray God that I may never have another mean act on my conscious. And I pray that God will help me conquer all that is bad in my disposition so that I may prove a blessing instead of a source of sorrow and uneasiness. As I know that I often am to Ma. If I could only keep the resolution that I make these pages would never again hear the record of such another scene as to day.

1. Alice was twenty-two years old in November 1864. She, like her sisters, eventually became an elementary-school teacher in Mississippi.

November the 15 Tuesday [1864]

I have not written any since the thread. And as it is rather late the events that has transpired during the interval must remain unwritten to night. Some few I must mention the first is I received a letter from Pauline yesterday. Leila was up hear Monday. She seemed in very good spirits, but some how I did not envy her quite much. I have lost some of the confidence [I] had in her. Ah well, none of us are perfect. And she might find the same fault of me.

January the 1 1865

It is now 10 o'clock and all is asleep but me. Yet, I can not for bear writing a few lines before retiring. The first night of the New Year. God grant that it may more of Happiness for us than the one just past. I am afraid to make resolutions for the year just entering for fear it may be like the past ones and I will not if can help it have it like them a score of broken promises. Our Christmas passed quietly enough. Our table lacked not many of its accoustomed luxeries; yet some how they were partaken of with the same zest as in former years. Ah, it is useless to sigh for the past. Things change evry year, aye evry day and we are of the world and must expect to bear its changes however sad. I wonder what pauline is doing to night. The boat came down so late that I did not get an opportunity to answer her letter. Mr. Miller[1] did not come up. It has been some time since he has been up here. I wonder if he has changed any. It has been so long since any one has been here that I dred the thought of a visit from any one. Ah well, I wonder where Mr Gardner and Mr Reed and the rest of them are to night though if reports be true they are at Savanah and the Confederacy has received another blow. Oh when will this cruel and bloody war end and how. We can only pray Gods will be done at termination. As why it was sent upon the land, none can tell. It is a subject that bafles me completely. Oh, the miserable thought that is conjured up by the mere mention of war.

1. James Miller, who lived in New Orleans, was Catharine's uncle.

January the 3 1865 Tuesday

Ah at last to night I have you to myself finaly. Emma[1] has been with us since last night. And Rose, Mag and Jean came up yester evening, took dinner with us and stayed until night and we had quite a lively little dance. But to day I was quite out of sorts. Em was here, but then she was not as lively as she used to be and the weather to is bad so I felt quite dull. Em was to have gone home early this morning, but we persuaded her to remain to our egg nogg drink which was to have been Monday night after New Year. We was unable to get any milk so was obliged until to night. So we was just about preparing to make it when Rosa Bennett[2] came running in and asked for anna. I believe I was seated at the piano when she came in. I asked her what she wants with her, but she gave me no answer, but continued on to the other rooms where Anna was seated talking to Ma. My curiosity was aroused and I a rose and followed her in to the room to ascertain her mission. She Kept on untill she came to Anna's chair when she threw her self into Annas lap [telling] Anna, Leila wants to know if you would have any objections to her bringing Mr Edward here. He has been teasing her to bring him and she has sent me to let you know. Anna mad[e] some slight objections to which Rosa paid no heed, but made herself quite easy. It was rather an announcement than anything else.

1. Emma Miller, the daughter of Adelia Johnson Miller and James Miller of New Orleans; she was Catharine's cousin.
2. A free woman of color and friend of Anna Johnson.

Saturday March the 4 1864 [1]

Bebe left today for New Orleans.[2]

1. This entry was most likely written in 1865.
2. Catharine's brother Benedict Byron Johnson. He left Natchez for New Orleans after being conscripted into the Black Mississippi Militia. Byron died in 1872; he, like his father, was shot and killed.

March the 5, 1865 Sunday

Today has been a dull one to me. How much I miss Bebe. He has only been gone one day yet the house is as still and dull as though some member of the family had died. I pray God he may return to us safely and shortly. For it seems to me the fate which takes him from us can do nothing worse. It seems so hard that those we love best and who are so necessary to our happiness we are all ways doomed to part from first. Ma is so much grieved at Bebes departure she says it is like a breaking up of the family. But I will try to look at things in a brighter light. Mrs Shavers[1] at the table this morning was speaking of him and her eyes filled with tears as she was telling us how she found Johnny[2] crying this morning about Bebe. Ah we may well be proud of him for he deserves all the love we can give him and more. I hear Clarence[3] coming in now I wonder where he has been all day. He will miss Bebes influence and I fear grow worse for the loss of it. Mr. McCary[4] when he was here this morning said that he had received a note from Bebe written just before the boat left the landing recommending him to rent out the shop[5] if he could get a good rent for it. He says he thinks it would be best. But I dont know what they will do with William for I think he will strenuously oppose any such measure. I am in hopes that it will not be necessary, that this thing will soon blow over and Bebe will come back and take possession himself. Jack and Mason[6] has been here all the morning. I spoke to Mason about the corn, but he would accept no pay. He made me a present of it and said that he considered himself under many obligations to the family and was willing to do any thing that he could for us. Jack wants me to let him have Kitty[7] but I dont think that it would be wise to do so for I dont like his treatment of her the last time he had her. He says that Byron gave him his saddle which I do not believe. I dont think Ma will let him have it untill she finds out from Bebe. For Jack talks too much to be relied on.

1. Mrs. Chavours, a friend of the family.
2. The son of William Johnson Jr.
3. Catharine's brother Clarence, born in May 1851.
4. Robert McCary, a free man of color of Natchez. He had been William Johnson Sr.'s friend, advisor, and hunting companion. He, like Johnson, had been born a slave. Like most of Natchez's other prosperous free people of color he was a mulatto, the child of James McCary, who was white, and one of his slave women. In 1813, when James McCary died, he emancipated his two female slaves, one of whom was the mother of his children, Robert and Kitty. James McCary's will is on file in the Adams County courthouse. Mary, Robert McCary's wife (who was also a mulatto and a free woman of color), was a close friend of Ann Johnson. Robert McCary remained a trusted advisor to the family after William's death.
5. The shop that Catharine refers to is the barbershop that had been owned previously by Catharine's father, William. At his death, two of his sons took over his trade.
6. Jack and Mason worked for the Johnsons.
7. Catharine's horse.

Saturday Night March the 11, 1865

A whole week is past and I have written none of its passing Events. And in some ways it has been an important one to me. Monday I arose early, it being my week to bake, and set about it with a good will. After baking quite a number of pies I sent Forest out with them. That day a number of trips had come down the River and landed here for awhile and they proved to be of a very reckless character. Well, I suppose Forest thought that he was doing for the best when he went among them, but in a short time he returned with out a single pie. They had taken every one from him. It was a real test to my patience but I hid it as well as I could and tryed not to murmur for I thought perhaps the disappointment was sent as a punishment for my rebellious repining a few days previous. Oh, how frantically do I try to overcome the bitter thoughts that strive for utterance. Yes, bitter and sinful thoughts that make my life a burden when I contrast the present with the past. I try to be content, but I often ask myself the question: why should the evil disposition of one person poison the whole family. Nevertheless, such is often the case. If it was not for William and his family, which he has brought here for us to provide for, our circumstances would be much better and the children might receive a chance of an education, which is their right. But instead of that, the burden of another family (for William does not provide for them) — and such a family — is a heavy weight on her slender income.[1] And prevents her giving them anything like an education. My heart swells with indignation and a bitter, bitter feeling of resentment towards him when I look at them and think for his sake they are growing up in ignorance. Poor Bebe he has nobly done his part and I pray that God will bless him where ever his fate may lead him. Now that he has gone, home does not seem like home with out him. Oh, how happy was that home once until William by his act made us all unhappy and since he has brought that woman here everything seems changed.[2] But I will write no more on the subject tonight.

Mr Wicker has been here nearly all day but we had our letters to write to day, I and Anna. So I was not in the parlor much. I do not like to go in company. I feel much happier when a lone. It is foolish I know, but it seems that I will have to get over this forbidden timidity that clings to me like second nature. I dont know but I have a presentment that my future will be an unhappy one and every year I grow more and more morbid. Ah me I wish I could be happy. Mr. Wicker brought Anna a beautiful bird and cage. The bird is a canary. A sweet little thing which he says he wants her to call Albert. I must close my journal for to night. It is late and all is sleeping but me.

1. Catharine is referring to Anna's slender income. Anna had become the de facto head of the household by 1865. Her mother was ill; William and Richard were not competent to hold that position; and Byron was gone.

2. "[T]hat woman" is William's wife. Her exact identity, however, remains elusive.

[Undated entry]

Sadly slowly the days creep by

Saturday June the 27th 1865

Paid today for one pair of shoes two dollars and six bits. $2.73.

Monday The First of May 1865 Natchez

I received a letter from Bebe this morning, but it contained nothing much of a gratifying character, that is concerning the shop. He said being absent from home so much lately he does not know hardly how to advise Ma. God knows it is a complicated matter and one that gives Ma considerable trouble for iff she allows the man to have the shop. Bebe says he might retain William[1] only untill he could gain possession and then discharge him to be a dead weight on Ma's hands; but that he could not be any more so, than he is now. Even iff he gives the promise to retain him, how could we hold him to that promise after he discovers that William is incompetent to fill any office however simple. Oh! it seems as if he will never regain his power of mind again. Never I fear. Bebe says that being unacquainted with affairs he is unable to judge in this case. Alas, dont he know William too well to suppose that things will prosper under his control. When he was here things were better for then his influence counteracted the evil effect of William's ways. Then the shop had support. Now it has only a weight and of course must follow a downward tendency. God knows where it will end. I can not bear the idea that bebe will not return and take his old place among us, or that he could be more contented away from home than at it. Yet when I consider I can not wonder much, that it should be so for he had so little inducement to remain. It is but natural that he should prefer to remain where he can live in the enjoyment of peace. Peace, I fear, it has fled our home forever. When memory invokes the past and I compare it with the present, the pictures are so different that my heart is filled with anguish, to think that we can never traverse the path of the beautiful past again. And sadly ask if we must tread the dark path that we are now pursuing throughout life. Oh! has the future nothing bright instow for us? I hope so, I trust so. I do not care to unravel much of the future. If my life's thread could end now, I would not repine. But every mortal has something of life's labor to perform and if I shrink from mine, God help me to do better.

1. William Johnson Jr. continued to work in the barbershop until he was fully incapacitated by his mental illness.

Sunday September the 24 1865

To day I feel a desire to write a sane record of some of the events that occur in our every day life. Yet, so unaccustomed am I to everything that I find the task of recording even plain everyday facts a hard one. William has been sick nearly all the week. I think that he came home sick on Thursday. Richard has not returned from the country where he went Wednesday. I guess it will be for the best if he does remain there for a while for he had begun to indulge in his old habit again. Man[1] went out in the country too. And without Ma's knowledge. She was very uneasy about him untill Bebe and Juanito[2] came home from the shop and told her that he saw Man in the company with Dan E. So we at once infered that he had Gone home with him. I am afraid that boy is destined to give Ma some trouble. yet, he is so headstrong. God knows we have had enough with Richard and William. The trouble that William brought us I fear will prove a lasting on[e]. He has become periodically insane. And she, each day her presance becomes more untolerable.[3] I have grown to hate her, and when I think of her as the author of all our troubles, it is almost death living under the same roof with her. I never thought that my heart could harbor such bitter feelings. Alas, how true it is that our natures are unknown. Even to ourselves untill tried by the fires of temptation and affiction. And in passing through the ordeal they are purified or hardened sometimes. I fear that the latter will be the result of my trial. But I hope that God will enable me to bear this trial patiently. And iff in after years it be removed I can look back and feel that I am better for the trial. Bebe has not come frome the shop yet and it now twenty five minutes past twelve. He has fallen into the habit lately of spending half of evry Sunday at the shop. It is a bad habit, but he quiets his conscience by saying that the spending of ones sabbeth in the persuit of gain is a general and not an individual sin. Some of Sicily's (our new servant) relations has sent for her. I hope that she will not leave us for though

slaves had

she is not very handy she seems willing and that goes a long ways to make one satisfied with a servant. And another thing, Sicily has grown very trifling and at time very insolent if it was not that Ma has had her so long she would soon set her a drift. I think it would come hard with us to part with Maria though.[4]

1. Clarence's son; short for "Little Man."

2. Juanito Garrus was a free man of color originally from Cuba. He took part interest in the management of the family plantations, Carthage and Black Lake. He also managed the family's barbershops, succeeding William and Richard. He and his brother Carlito worked for and even lived with the Johnsons.

3. Catharine is speaking of William Jr.'s wife.

4. Sicily and Maria had been two of the Johnson's slaves. Catharine's seemingly contradictory remarks about Sicily being "our new servant" and her being with her mother "so long" might suggest a change in the status of the women. They had been the family's slaves but by 1865 would have been freed and thus been considered servants.

Monday Sep 25 1865

I think that we will have some rain soon. It is so warm. Richard and Man came home last night. Richard said he left all well. Man, as I supposed, went out to see about those pigs. This morning when I got up I felt worried and discontented somehow and my head ached too. I never feel happy and contented now. That feeling seems to have fled forever. I went down to my breakfast feeling peevish and was just in the mood to speak crossly if misunderstood. Juanito had not come to breakfast yet and Gramma[1] kept telling me to clear off the table and I spok rather abruptly. Well there was nothing in my words so much than my manner was rather huffish. Well I am sorry but then I felt so bad. And Gramma has grown rather fault finding here lately. She seems to have changed as much since that woman came here. There is William just come up on the gallery. Laughing and grumbling to himself as is habit here lately. He seldom if ever has any sane moments now and sometimes makes use of very ugly expressions at the table. As he did this morning I wish so much that he could be put under medical treatment. I received a letter from Pauline this morning.

1. Catharine is writing of her grandmother Harriett Battles, who had lived with the family for most of Catharine's life.

Monday Night [1]

The boys has not come yet. I wonder what detains them so long. Juanito seemed somewhat depressed to day. We all tryed to find out the cause, but without success. I think his depression was caused by the strange actions of the Old man.[2] He dont understand him as we do. I received a letter from R.B. this evening which somewhat surprised me in as much as they have kept so close lately. I had begin to think that they had given us up.

1. This entry is undated, but it was probably written in 1865.
2. Family papers in Natchez and Baton Rouge and judicial and property records in New Orleans suggest that the elder white William Johnson, who had originally owned Amy Johnson and Adelia and William, remained close to the family. In the 1851 Register of Free People of Color in New Orleans he is listed as the white patron of James Miller. He was still alive in the 1860s and is probably the "Old man" to whom Catharine refers.

Natchez February Monday The 5 1866

I shall not begin my writing to night with complaints though the old heart sickness is upon me. I have been feeling sad and strange all day. Tho' that is nothing. I suppose that feeling was brought on by the disagreeable events that transpired this morning. William was in one of his moods this morning, abusing Gramma shamefully and in a very improper manner when Richard spoke to him about it. But his interferance only had the effect of turning the tide of abuse on himself. Richard became very angry and went off and had him arrested. But they only kept him confined a short time as they released him at dinner. I dont know what is ever to become of him.

March the First 1866, Wednesday

It has been sometime since I have written any in my book. I am with that as with everything else, careless and neglectful. Oh me I would give anything for just one peep into the future. But if my prognostications be realized, my future will be very sad. I do not like the mood into which I am falling so gloomy and distrustful. I am never happy now. I think if I would think less of my owwn defects and devote more of my time to self culture and to promoting the happiness of others I would thereby increase my own happiness. But I am so hopeless of succeeding in anything, if I make resolutions to day I break them tomorrow. And thus it will be throughout my life. Oh! I feel now the bitter punishment that follows neglected hours.

Juanito has been to New Orleans and just returned yesterday. He has been absent nine days. Jimmy came up with him, and [Juanito] brought each of us a ring for our Christmas gifts. And for Jener[1] he brought a ring and a pair of Earrings. Ours was a ring with two hearts. But Jeners was a plain gold. I think he intended it as engagement ring. Poor fellow he was doomed to disappointment. They were both in the parler a long time and when he came out I noticed that his manner was restless and his voice sounded hoarce and unnatural. I spoke to him, asking if he had a cold. I dont know he replied. They tell me it is consumption, if so I wish it would soon complete its work. I told him that it was wrong to talk that way. I cant help it. I allways speak what I think. But you should not when you think wrong. He stood about for awhile as if lost in thought with a wild look about his eyes that I never noticed before. Then I spoke to him asking him when he was coming to see us again. I dont know he replied perhaps not for sometime. Or perhaps I shall come Monday as I expect to leave for up the river soon.[2]

1. Eugenia Johnson, one of Catharine's younger sisters.
2. Evidently Eugenia changed her mind about Juanito. They married August 23, 1873, and had several children — among them, Clement, Alphonse, Arthur, and Hukey.

March[1]

It is nearly eight Oclock in the evening and I am all alone and perhaps shall be so for several hours. All are gone out to a meeting called the sorrow Lodge. It is so lonely I almost wish now that I had gone. Just through mere caprice and willfulness I deprived myself from witnessing an interesting sight. And one that I may never have another opportunity of witnessing. But it is too late now. I felt cross yesterday and said I would not go. When Anna assigned a motive for my not going which was not in a reality a correct one or rather the principal one. I admit that the one she gave did add to my disposition to remain at home. But be as it may when she spoke I got angry and vowed that I would not go [in] pride or some other feeling.

1. This entry is undated, but it was probably written in 1866.

Wednesday May the 30 1866

How my head aches. I have been feeling bad all day. As I do not feel like writing I thought that I would — see how my mind wanders. I meant to say I did not feel like sewing, and would write some. Since last I wrote many changes has taken place. Yes, even in that short time. For when last I wrote, poor William was still at home. But now he is far away confined in an insane asylum. But I pray that his reason may soon be restored and poor Mrs Shavours, her place too is vacant. Dear God's messenger came and she went out from among us never more to return. I trust that she has found a home, brighter and happier than any mortal gifts could render this poor earthly one. How dull it is now and nearly everyone in the house is complaining. And I am sure we all look miserable. Juanito's brother came up last thursday. He look very young. I dont think that he resembles Juanito much. The day after his arrival Juanito, Man, and Richard went to the place and while there they went in swimming and Juanito came near drowning. Man caught him in his hair as he was going down the last time and Richard and him together brought him ashore. It would have been a sad sad thing had he got drowned. This morning while Man was in market he got into some difficulty with that boy of Ben Dixon's and he went home and told his Father and he came after Man and hauled him near the corner and began with him about his boy. Man attempted to explain, but he would listen to no explanations, but kept up a great noisy abuse. Just then Bibe came along and hearing the name that he applied to Man, ordered him to give ben a brick. He applyed the same name to bibe. He sooner done than bibe make a brick fly at him, which made Ben scamper calling out as he ran. I did'ent call you that name. I did'ent call you that name. I guess he will not mettle aggin soon with them.

My head aches and I feel so unhappy. It seems that the times grow harder instead of better and I do so dread poverty. And another thing every body seems so changed and most of all I grieve over the change that has taken place in my self. To the present, the past seems so Bright. So bright that I dare not call up its memories, for it makes me wretch to think that in reality I can never live them again. And I know that it is wrong, but sometimes I do long to die. I feel so useless and so hopeless. I strugle for the wright but my strength and nature are both weak and fail me in the strugle. God help me for I know not what I shall do.

Monday July 25, 1866

Ann came to day to live with us. I hope that she may be satisfied to remain here thus she may continue to please us.[1]

1. "Ann" is not Ann Johnson, Catharine's mother. She was living in the household already, and she in fact died in 1866.

Sunday Night July 29 1866

On Tuesday night about 12 OClock Mr McCary Died of Apoplexy. I know that he is gone. Yet, I can not realise it, that he is the best friend that we had on earth is gone. Oh if he could only have been spared to us a few more years longer.

Monday Sept. 1866

For the first time since Ma's death I take up my pen to write. But Oh how hard I find the task. Even now, I cannot realiz that she is gone from us forever. Four weeks yesterday Since they buried her in the grave. Oh if I was only prepared how gladly would i lay dow by her side. But I can not realiz that Ma, our patient loving Mother is gone.

Friday October the 5 1866

I have been ironing all day to day and have nothing of importance to write. In fact, I have that at no times. Tene went down home Wednesday which was the third of the month. I felt sorry to part from her for somehow I like her better this time then I ever did before. She seemed truer and more attatched to us. And an other thing her kindness to poor William wiped out all that was dissagreeable in the past. Poor William. I wonder if we will ever see him perfectly restored to reason. I fear not. Oh! I should like to see him home once more after our sad sad loss.

I had mine and we were happy
Riding in a sleigh sleigh
Riding in a sleigh

CHILDHOOD

I Visit The Scene of My Childhood.
I came to the spot where oft I had strayed
In the days of my youth in childhood's sweet bloom
The friends that I loved had passed to their graves
And the place wore a look of sadness and gloom.

2nd V
The moss covered cot by the mountain's loved
Where a fond doting mother taught me to pray
Weired — like and silent loomed up to my gaze
Begrimed with the debris and dust of decay
The mountain's steep side in dark waving pine
Still towered aloft as in days that are gone

Monday July 1 1872

Catharine Samuels came to me to school this morning. I wish that a half a dozen more of my scholars would come and then it would not be so tiresome.

She seem to be dull but good natured. I must study hard myself so that I will be ready should they call upon me to teach again. I do hope sincerely that I may be selected for then I could help them at home so much as of now I am helpless. Ockie and Leana has gone to the country. I wonder how long they will stay. I hope not long for then I cannot say my lessons so well.

Natchez June 1873

It has been a long long time since I have written anything in the pages of this book. Since then we have suffered wrong in every shape. I can not bring my self to write of the horrors of that time. Twice has death entered our family snatching away at once the most useful and the best. O Friends we have lost by worse than death — estrangement.[1] All our boys are vanishing fast. Soon the ties that binds us on earth will indeed be few.

1. By June 1873 Byron Johnson had died.

Through long long years to seek, to strive, to yearn,
    For human love and never quench that thirst.
    To pour the soul out winning no return,
    Our fragile idol by delusions nursed,
    On things that falter, and by need to lean,
    To mourn the changed, the far away, the dead,
    To send our troubled spirits through the unseen,
    Intensely questioning for treasures fled.

Monday 1873

I received a letter from Thomas Coleman to day. Anna received one also. It the first letter that I have received for years and I scarcely know how to answer it. But I suppose that I will make the attempt even if I fail which I don't think that I will.

I saw poor Dr. Inge Just now. How care worn he looks. They tell me that he has applied for rations. How sad that must be to a spirit like his. God help us all. We, none of us, know what fate has in store for us so all that we can do is to wait patiently for the slow uplifting of the vail hidest the future. We can but mourn the past, the fare away the day and sader than all the changed, the living dead. I call them for they are indeed dead to us. Change is sometimes worse than death. I wonder if fate has much more that is sad in store [the rest of this entry is illegible]

[Undated entry]

I sit down this 29 night of June to scrible a few wretched thoughts. For wretched I say they must be. For tonight, I am as wretched a soul as lives in this world. The times are so hard and seem to be growing worse every day. I believe that to all our other ills and troubles is to be added that of poverty. For every year we grow poorer and poorer. We can't get our rents and for two terms I have toiled in the Public School and received nothing but a lot of worthless warrants for my pain.[1] Anthony tells me that they have almost concluded to fund them. I wonder if I will be benefited by the act. If payment of them is postponed for six years God only knows where I will be in that time.

1. Catharine began teaching in the Union School in Natchez in 1872. She taught there on and off until she finally moved to Ravenwood and began teaching there. She is complaining in the letter of being paid in warrants. These warrants were issued by the school board and often proved to have little value.

June 21 1874

We had quite a hard rain yesterday which was accompanied with hail, lightening and thunder. The lightening was so vivid that we took refuge in bed from its flashes. We will be late in school this morning for Johnson has come for a settlement and I well know that it will be some time before Anna gets through. Oh, is nothing but a call for money all the time.

[Undated entry][1]

The Shop we had failed us. Had any person in the world told me that Carlito would ever have changed as he has, I would not have believed it. God help him and forgive me if any act of mine has made him take one step on the path to ruin. It seems to me there is none true in this world.

1. This undated entry was probably written in 1874.

[Undated entry][1]

I receive a letter from W. to day. but instead of giving pleasure there was something about the time that give me pain. He began as usual only calling me sister. But there was an air of constraint about it that should not be a found in a brother's letter. It seemed to be written under the conciouness that he was writing to one who could not understand a serious thought or sentiment. In fact, as though he was writing to a little simple child. One who could understand nothing but the barest noncense. I dont wonder at it however for I have ever played the fool in his presence. Or, perhaps it was written in another sense. I mean if he can be absurd enough to think that I can have another love for him than that of a sister. And is afraid of giving me encouragement. If I could be certain that he thought so I am afraid I should hate him. But no, I will not wrong him by thinking that he wrongs me that way. He thinks that I am the simple foolish child in reality that by action have given him wright to think. Ah well, I must try and discourage him and act with more sense. Then then I will not have cause to complain of the treatment of others toward me. Well it is getting late — I must go to bed — good night old book.

1. This undated entry also was probably written in 1874.

Life has a burden for every ones shoulders
None can escape from its trouble and care
Miss it in youth and 'twill come when we are older
And fits us as close as the garments we wear

Life has a burden for every ones shoulders
None may escape from its trouble and care
Miss it in youth and 'twill come when we are older
And fit us as close as the garments we wear

Oh I have sinned and I have suffered
More than words of mine can tell
And in sorrow I am returning
To the home I loved so well.
Oh! I little knew how precious
Were the simple precious home
Til from paths of light and duty
Way ward feet had learned to roam.

Oh how vain was I to follow,
Where the hand of danger led.
Dazzled by the dreams of splender

Till from paths of wright had fled
God forgive me for the sorrow.
I have cause them one and all
He will hear my poor petition
For he heeds the sparrow's fall.

THINKING THINKING EVER THINKING

Thinking Oh! I'm ever thinking
And my heart is beating light,
As alone I sit in silence,
In my room again to night; And my heart
Backward o'er my girlhood pathway is beating
I am ***** ***** to love
When the dreamy spell comes o'er me
Which I cannot help but love
Fairest hopes I cherished warmly

In the days so swiftly flown
Still afar are all things from me
Which my faith has ever grown.
Strugling on with noble effort
Never tarrying on the way
I have golden sheaves of promise
In the future brightening day.

In the future brightening day
In the future brightening day
In days so swiftly flown
In days so swiftly flown.

✣ Epilogue

Anna and Catharine wrote letters, one to the other, during the final years of the nineteenth century. Catharine retired from teaching just before the turn of the twentieth century and moved from Ravenwood back to the old family home on State Street in Natchez. Anna continued to teach at the Union School in Natchez until 1906, when she retired. After her retirement, she moved to Peachland, a plantation that was located just a few miles north of Natchez. Anna and her brother Clarence sharecropped the plantation with several local families. Anna rarely left Peachland after she moved there. Her niece Mary Louise Miller, in a recent interview, says that she and the rest of the family would go to visit Anna at Peachland on Sundays. Occasionally, Anna would leave the plantation to visit Catharine and her other surviving brothers and sisters and nieces and nephews at the old family home in Natchez.

Catharine died in 1901 in the family home. She is buried near her father, William T. Johnson, and her grandmother, Amy Johnson, in the cemetery of the Natchez Cemetery Association. Despite the fact that Anna was the eldest daughter, she lived on past her brothers and sisters until 1916. She died in Natchez, where she had gone after her last illness; she was returned to Peachland for burial. The Johnson family of Natchez continues today through the legacy of Dr. William R. Johnston. He was the grandson of William T. Johnson and Ann Battles Johnson, and the son of Clarence. Dr. Johnston attended Wilberforce College and Howard University. He returned to Natchez to practice medicine after his graduation. His niece, Mary Louise Miller, is presently living in Yazoo City, Mississippi.

Even though the family persisted mostly intact throughout the nineteenth century, conditions changed dramatically for them. Having found its roots in the freedom of Amy Johnson and Harriett Battles, the large extended Johnson-Miller family grew and prospered under the care and guidance of Amy and Harriett's daughters, Adelia and Ann. Yet, despite their best intentions, the two branches of the family, the Millers in Louisiana and the Johnsons in Mississippi, grew apart. The financial difficulties brought on by the Civil War and Reconstruction evidently proved to be too much for the family. Each branch slowly lost touch. All of Adelia's surviving children in New Orleans married, had children of their own, and moved away. Few of Ann's children married. Of her nine surviving children, it appears that only William, Eugenia, and Clarence married. Ann's children faced different conditions in Natchez than did Adelia's in New Orleans. These relatively well-educated affluent free people of color would have had fewer choices of partners in Natchez.

What the Natchez branch of the family faced during the eras of Reconstruction and Jim Crow, when formal distinctions between free and unfree vanished, were extreme economic hardship and harsh racism. Despite their many difficulties, however, the younger Johnson women, Anna, Catharine, Alice, and Josephine, rejected what many other free people of color chose, which was to distance themselves entirely from freed slaves in order to distance themselves as completely as possible from racism. Instead, these women committed themselves to the freed slaves. The sisters worked with these freed slaves and their children every day as their teachers. Their brothers continued as barbers and farmers, hiring freed slaves and working in the fields with them. It was this legacy that the family passed along to its heirs. Dr. William R. Johnston returned to Natchez to continue the legacy his family had established before him, to care for his people. Mary Louise Miller is a retired school teacher. Her daughter, Lois Hawthorne, teaches school today in Gulfport, Mississippi.

Index